SLY DEEDS

Performance Texts
by
Nigel Wells

Edited, with Director's Notes, by David Ian Rabey

Afterword by Clive Meachen

Print ISBN 978-1-0687077-4-2

Published by
Llyfrau Cambria Books, Wales, United Kingdom.
Cambria Books and Cambria Stories are imprints of Cambria Publishing Ltd.
Discover our other books at: www.cambriabooks.co.uk

ABOUT THE AUTHOR AND CONTRIBUTORS

Nigel Wells received Arts Council of Wales book prizes for *The Winter Festivals* (Bloodaxe Books, 1980) and *Wilderness/Just Bounce* (Bloodaxe Books, 1989). He received an Arts Council of Wales bursary for *Walesland/Gwaliadir* (Gomer, 2006: with a parallel Welsh translation by Caryl Lewis).

David Ian Rabey is a director, dramatist and actor, and Emeritus Professor of Theatre and Theatre Practice at Aberystwyth University, where he taught 1985-2020.

His critical monographs include *Howard Barker: Politics and Desire* (1989, 2020), *David Rudkin: Sacred Disobedience* (1997), *English Drama Since 1940* (2003), *Howard Barker: Ecstasy and Death* (2009), *The Theatre and Films of Jez Butterworth* (2015), *Theatre, Time and Temporality* (2016), and *Alistair MacDowall's* Pomona (2018).

His plays for Lurking Truth Theatre Company/ Cwmni'r Gwir sy'n Llechu include two published volumes, *The Wye Plays* (2004) and *LoveFuries* (2008); and *Land of My Fathers* (staged 2018) and *Last Ditch (Anhrefn yng Nghymru)* (staged 2023).

Clive Meachen is a former lecturer in American Literature and Film at Aberystwyth University. He has written on Charles Olsen, Robert Creeley and Don DeLillo.

Front cover painting: *Sly-Deeds-Ark* by Paul Martinez Frias.

Poster prints by Emma Taylor

Wordskill by Alan Halsey

CONTENTS

Introductory Approach, and A Director's Reflections on *Resurrection Men* 1

    1: 'Teeming emptiness' 1

    2. *Resurrection Men*: Telling the Times 4

RESURRECTION MEN 9

'Alphabet, Delusion, Portent, Music': A Director's Reflections on *That Slidey Dark* 49

THAT SLIDEY DARK 55

'Simultaneous Solitudes': A Director's Reflections on *Skin Shanty* 87

SKIN SHANTY 93

Word*s*kill: *The Glory Reel,* and beyond… 155

    1. *The Glory Reel*: pain to stop the pain 155

    2. Sailing to Walesland/Gwaliadir 157

THE GLORY REEL 159

SLY DEEDS: an Afterword 209

References 214

Introductory Approach, and A Director's Reflections on *Resurrection Men*

David Ian Rabey

1: 'Teeming emptiness'

My section title, above, is drawn from the last line in Nigel Wells's poem *Wilderness* (Wells 1988: 27), which provides an apt place from which to begin. In 1991, I was invited to direct a small-scale theatre performance based on *Wilderness*, as an event presented as part of a sequence of 'Verbals' – a series of readings and performances initiated by Clive Meachen and Douglas Houston in collaboration with Aberystwyth Arts Centre.

Wilderness is a poem which summons imagined voices from the margins of American historical, literary and musical mythologies, reincarnated by Wells to pursue their doomed wars of independence in the ritual form of a ghost dance. Although separated by time and other social conventions of perception, these voices interpenetrated each other, in their strange distinctions, rages, separations and invocations: their energies combining in Wells's form. To adapt the text for performance, Wells prepared a vocal orchestration which divided the poem between four disparate (often mutually qualifying) voices, thus avoiding the simple and simplistic 'one-performer-per-character' format and mobilizing a crosscurrent of perspectives.

To devise an appropriately accompanying physical score, I encouraged my four performers (Jon Lever, Mandy Lumsden, Jamie Rance, Charmian Savill) to work in pairs (in all possible permutations) on each section and voice, to seek out, improvise upon, and express physical actions and gestural imagery which Wells's words generated in their imaginations. After group discussion to identify the most striking initiatives, I led a process of selection, montage and development of these physical dynamics, to create an interactive flow of energies of spoken language, movement and spatial relations. These energies could thus be purposefully identified into an agreed and objective score, as a basis for the performed re-creation (not imitation) of expressive tensions discovered through rehearsal.

1

The performers' physical and vocal score gained a further dimension with the simultaneous devising of a musical one, played live by two versatile, imaginative and sensitive musicians, Nick Jones and Nick Taylor, in response to what they witnessed. With the supporting frameworks of these parallel scenic scores, the performers could pursue the pleasurable dangers of making their imaginative matrix work for them anew, fully vitalized to the possibilities of discovery and mutual surprise generated by maximum concentration and precision between selves, words, and others. Wells's poetry demands no less than contact with each word – in some cases, each syllable – and I exhorted the performers to reach for this: to sing and dance out the mutual excoriation, at the same time listening to and responding to each note and word and movement in every other performance, building a feedback loop of energy and riding its momentum. My other principal exhortation to performers was to discover and express sensual pleasure in the arias of language being offered them, and in the operatic range of sensations they reflected – from grief to despair to desire to the savagery of parasitic leeching to the ecstasy of being leeched – with a view to disclosing all the simultaneous and contrary pressures of attraction/reclamation and repulsion/abjection inherent in a kernel couplet in the first section of *Wilderness*:

Oh horrible grace

'You are our child' (Wells 1988: 2)

In the various scenes of *Wilderness*, as in the subsequent texts gathered here, there is a frequent oscillation between the totemic and the ironic. Faustian determination is undercut by crippling enervations. Inscrutable, irreducible force acquires form and energy. Forensic would-be analysts try to limit, and account for, the invisible find that their descriptive efforts and tools break down in the face of undefinable forces. Sexuality is figured as possessive and deliberately sacrilegious, a *pas de deux* of challenge and revenge, a tango of striving and defiance, with parallel insistences resolving into irresolvable separateness. Finally, and characteristically, in *Wilderness* the last surviving native American of his tribe is encased, yet remains dissociative, even in disintegration: the last of several terminal images.

I have dwelt thus on the challenges of *Wilderness* because they provided me with an alien and unforeseeable set of propositions, situations, processes and images to explore, which nevertheless yielded discoveries which would inform and equip me for my directorial grapplings with most of the subsequent Wells texts collected in this volume. Wells's writing makes demands which are initially apparently paradoxical, but which can become increasingly and disturbingly logical through rehearsal. These demands on the performers can be identified thus:

That they be true to the sense, and be true to the strangeness, of each voice and each moment, expressing rather than explaining.

That they make every effort to communicate that strangeness, notwithstanding the knowledge of the impossibility of complete understanding, indeed the more so because of it (as in Beckett, Rudkin and Barker's drama).

That they be disturbing in their singular coherence and compel belief in their otherness: all Wells personae are isolated, and usually marginalized, for being uniquely true to their own codes of living, speaking and being.

In summary: these performance texts work to demonstrate that the dominant social, and individual, terms of definition of possibilities are neither complete nor exhaustive. Thematically and theatrically, they involve what Eugenio Barba terms the interweaving of parallel, or 'twin', logics, without substituting one for the other, or permitting dominance:

> Logic – that is, a series of motivated and consequent transitions – can exist even if it is secret, incommunicable, even when its rules cannot extend beyond a single individual's horizon [...] What we call irrationality might be the (inconsequent) oscillation left to the mechanical repetition of our fixations and obsessions which disappear and reappear, agitatedly, without development. But it might also be a rationality which is *ours* alone, a *raison d'être* which does not help us to be understood but to communicate with ourselves. (Barba, in Barba and Savarese, 1991: 60)

Mechanical objectivism would outlaw such relationships in the theatre of each individual's sense of self, to enclose its wildernesses. Wells's texts provide a dramatic figuring of contrary tendencies towards the problematically reflective in what *Wilderness* significantly identifies as 'the soul (that crowded isolate)' (Wells 1988: 10).

2. *Resurrection Men*: Telling the Times

Coincidentally, during our rehearsal period for Wells's *Resurrection Men*, a similarly titled book appeared. Brian Bailey's historical study, *The Resurrection Men: A History of the Trade in Corpses* (1991), provides documentary information about the distinctively British practice of bodysnatching in general, and about the notorious case of Billy Burke and William Hare in particular. The case subsequently inspired a film, *Burke and Hare* (directed by John Landis, 2010), and its further resonances form the subject of Caroline McCracken-Flesher's *The Doctor Dissected: A Cultural Autopsy of the Burke and Hare Murders* (2011).

Bailey observes how the incentivization of secretive exhumation, as a profitable business, was a significant paradigm of the expediencies on which the self-congratulatory "civilization" of Georgian Britain was based; it also provides an example of how every society 'suffers' (and generates?) 'the crime it deserves' (Bailey 1991: 19). Bailey elaborates, and suggests that, in an age of obsessive materialism, the activities of grave-robbers (euphemistically dubbed 'resurrection men') reflected a generally presumed cheapness of life, even as they arguably represented a necessary evil in an age when medical research was inhibited by the connected pieties of religious sentimentality and economic repression:

> The motive was financial: the opportunity was presented by the state of medical knowledge and research (governmentally impoverished); the method was made easy by the appalling condition of urban churchyards. (Bailey 1991: 6)

Nevertheless, a tacit professional trade in corpses, for scientific dissection and analysis, might have been tolerated in limited and discrete forms, were it not for the maverick developments of Burke and Hare, who 'muscled in on the scene and brought the curtain down by going too far' (Bailey: 165).

Thus, the trade, material and existence of the resurrection men fundamentally problematized the assurances and language of British society: they literally, professionally and criminally re-presented the disruptive effects which Julia Kristeva identifies as 'The Abject'. In brief, 'The Abject' is how Kristeva describes:

> Something rejected from which one does not part […] It is thus not lack of cleanliness or health that causes abjection but what disturbs identity, system, order. What does not respect borders, positions, rules. The in-between, the ambiguous, the composite. The traitor, the liar, the criminal with a good conscience […] the killer who claims he is a saviour. (Kristeva, 1982: 4)

4

These disturbing qualities characterize the dramatic hinterland, momentum and power of all of Wells's texts for performance. Kristeva further characterizes the reflexive process which she associates with attempted abjection: the subject, 'weary of fruitless attempts to identify with something on the outside', discovers the ostensibly impossible *within*: indeed, the subject 'finds that the impossible constitutes its very *being*' (Kristeva, 1982: 5). This triggers, in the social and/or individual discourse of cohesion, attempts to repress and deny this offensive and infectious symptom. However, as Kristeva notes, attempts will prove manifestly and significantly imperfect: 'Curious primacy, where what is repressed cannot really be held down, and where what represses always already borrows its strength and authority from what is apparently very secondary: language' (*ibid.*, 13-14).

The script of Wells's *Resurrection Men* avoids stage directions, apart from the injunctions to Jamie to mimic the voices of the other characters in his penultimate action. This licenses all working to present the text to develop their own 'score', a selective collage of their own most vital physical and spatial responses to the language. I will offer some impressions of our 1992 premiere staging for information, rather than as prescription.

Rehearsals for *Resurrection Men* – and, indeed, for the subsequent *That Slidey Dark* and *Skin Shanty* – followed the same initial process as those for *Wilderness*. All four performers worked, in permutations of pairs, on the speedily improvised generation of physical and gestural images in response to each section of the text. I would then lead a process of selection, "cutting and pasting", juxtaposing and assembling the strongest images into a choreographic flow. The objective was to provide suggestive, surprising and contrapuntal actions which were spatially and interactively 'poetic' rather than literally enactive of the events described. The intention was to provide actions which metaphorically dilated the associations of the language, avoiding wherever possible a reduction to a single meaning.

Our early reference points in the gestation of the production of *Resurrection Men* were the folk ballad and the mummers' play. The latter is deliberately evoked by the traditional self-introduction of several characters: 'In comes I'. A ritual folklore presentation style, powerful in the primacy of its colours, suits the play very well (an English analogue might be provided by John Arden's 1959 play *Serjeant Musgrave's Dance*). However, this was augmented by other aesthetic and stylistic references: we opted to evoke the would-be sobrieties of black suits and white shirts for costume, skewed by grotesque and macabre black-and-white face make-up redolent of German Expressionism and Weimar cabaret, which also informed a consciously presentational form of performance. The only splashes of visual colour were provided by the two musicians (Nick Jones and Nick Taylor, here collectively designated 'Brouhaha'), dressed as pied and pixilated street buskers, striking up an overture and subsequently weaving in and out of the action. In accordance with the folklore ritual and mummers' play affinities, and in deference to the likely familiarity of the case of Burke and Hare, the production obviated suspense and introduced an element of foreboding by using a hangman's rope: both as running visual motif and multi-purpose prop. For example, Jamie sang the opening song whilst holding, with Knox, the rope for Burke and Hare to skip over – a motif evoking a childhood game, which they would reverse in their chorus, by using the rope to wind in Jamie and truss him up. Indeed, we incorporated several active foreshadowings of Jamie's fate and Hare's betrayal of Burke to enhance the folk ballad sense of inevitability, in which the tragic extends into the robustly archetypal and is neither limited nor debilitating. Rather, the characters are unrepentantly reflective and decidedly demonstrative of apparently typical action (to scapegoat or betray; to accept scapegoating or betrayal), which they play out to the hilt, and beyond. It is their energy in doing so (rather than a startling dramatic reversal) that is exhilarating and disturbing.

Indeed, childrens' games provided several bases for choreography, as suggested by the text's evocations of ballad rhyme and doggerel street chants. After having been used as an "anatomical model" for Dr Knox's demonstrations, Jamie found himself thrown centrally into a game of "piggy-in-the-middle" between Burke and Hare for the 'middleman' chant. This then morphed into a game of blind man's bluff for the second stanza; and finally, on the line 'Cut up the middleman', the configuration of a trust circle took on a shocking twist as Burke and Hare mimed an incision up Jamie's torso and a stretching open of his ribs into a "blood eagle" configuration, turning Jamie's last syllable, 'man', into a scream of pain. But this was, for the character of Jamie, an isolated non-sequential moment and image, like his adoption of a standardized, cultured 'paper voice' in which to deliver exposition. Jamie characteristically squealed gleefully at most things – including jokes, of which he was the butt – until the end. If the character of Jamie has a posthumous apotheosis, it is in his consciousness of his position as totemic sacrifice, and his sensed ability to 'tell the times' from that perspective.

As will be apparent from the cast list, all performers, except Ian Staples as Burke, were female, attired in male drag. This again evoked the subversions of Weimar cabaret and constituted a further source of disquieting power. In her scenes with Burke, Bridget Keehan infused the role of Hare with a homoerotic seductiveness and profoundly ambiguous allure. Hare's switching of loyalties to The Judge was also lent a sexual resonance by their thoroughly physicalized and apparently pleasurable entwinement; and Hare's last farewell to Burke suggested a *film noir* ambience in its androgynous echo of a *femme fatale* revealing a toying affection and sexual excitement even as their prey was consigned to his fate. Hare's duplicitous vindictiveness provides a powerful springboard to the Burke performer to resolve to hold fast to his dignity, with baleful defiance, in his last speech.

Nick Jones and Nick Taylor provided stirring original folk-styled compositions for the songs, as well as playing an individual 'theme' whereby each character could be re/introduced; subsequently, this theme could be modulated to reflect events and moods. Jones and Taylor also supplied rhythmic colourings for the enunciation of sections of the text: notably a slow, loping, wryly menacing reggae beat on a bongo for the section in 'Who Killed Cock Robin' metre, against which the performers could make their interjections in a rap/toast style (the work of Linton Kwesi Johnson was my own personal reference point here). Jones distinguishes his own composition work for this production (compared to the subsequent Wells texts) as less structured melodically (outside of the central ballads), more improvised with and from rehearsal, to provide pace and ambience.

I record a few other set-pieces of choreography, to give a sense of the production's atmosphere and agility. Louise Tickle was the performer required to demonstrate the most protean mobility. Whereas the performers of the roles of Burke, Hare and Jamie were principally involved in presenting a single character, Louise played not only Dr Knox, but also the roles of Inspector, Advocate, Judge, and Murder Victims (the incidental "normal people"). For the litany of murder victims, Charmian Savill, the performer playing Jamie, would establish a physical posture to characterize each entrant: Louise would assume this, regarding then mimicking Charmian/Jamie as if a reflection in a full-length mirror. Louise would then have her speech as that assumed character of Murder Victim interrupted by their sudden death spasm, often involving a stretch into a grotesque posture of death (suggesting strangulation, battery, evisceration) while remaining literally untouched. On the other side of the stage, the performers of Burke and Hare enacted the relevant murder technique on each other, as if in a rough playground game by gleefully competitive children. Jamie registered his first moment of surprise, doing a "double take", when the time came for Louise to enact Jamie's own murder. As Jamie leaned further into the scene in bewilderment, Louise grabbed his hand to catapult him into the tableau to assume the Victim's position. Louise would later attempt to establish contact with Jamie, as if to pull him out of the position again ('Jamie, don't leave Jamie / Don't go off with death') – unsuccessfully. After death, Jamie's face was distended into a rictus grin, his 'nearly face', by Knox's probing fingers: and Jamie maintained this ghastly expression when he began to speak, beyond Knox's control, to express his posthumous rhapsody of wonder. This manually assisted "smiley" rictus grin was deployed as a motif elsewhere in the production, most notably by Hare stretching out Burke's mouth at the end of his farewell, on the word 'irony'.

The performers were underlit and sidelit by an arrangement of anglepoise lamps: a swift and cheap practical exigency, for performance in a space with no lighting rig (Aberystwyth Arts Centre foyer, arranged in cabaret seating). The lamps cast long sharp shadows, which contributed further to the expressionist mood and effectively enhanced the eeriness of scenic tableaux. One juncture featured the emergence of a physicalized and malign Warped Justice (at the section beginning 'From where the world is slowing'), constructed from three bodies entwined into a nightmarishly ambulant totem pole, also gesturally evoking the proverbial three monkeys who professed to hear, see and speak no evil. This totem incorporated Jamie, with a predatory embrace and a forcing of the disfiguring rictus grin (on 'got to smile'). The physicalized image of the malign totem was subsequently evoked when, after mutual flirtation, Hare jumped onto the back of The Judge (on the line 'who will atone?'). The "blinding" of Justice – the sense of associative interlocking (self-)mutilation – was further suggested by Knox miming the surgical removal of the other performers' eyeballs during his apologia.

The most shameless directorial "dressing" occurred at the end. Finally alone, amidst the other characters' silence, Jamie animated their bodies and parodied their voices, as if they were abandoned puppets, run-down toys or waxworks in The Chamber of Horrors. In further defiance of their silence, Charmian, the performer of Jamie, produced a knife and a genuine ox heart (sourced from a local butcher's shop) which she viciously quartered (on the line 'intended to mitigate the force of the heart's action'). After speaking the words 'the tale's complete', Jamie then picked up the pieces of the quartered heart and tried to make fit back together again, like a cheeky vandal who was suddenly suffused with regret that a dangerous game of copycat destruction has broken something irrevocably. After the line, 'and Jamie's ghost is obsolete', was delivered in a tone of dawning realization, the segments of the heart were permitted to slither apart from Jamie's grasp, to hit the stage in a succession of wet slaps. Knox's elusive enigma – 'the substance of the heart' – was thus given terrible playful immediacy, as the final visual image, and sounding.

RESURRECTION MEN

A Ballad

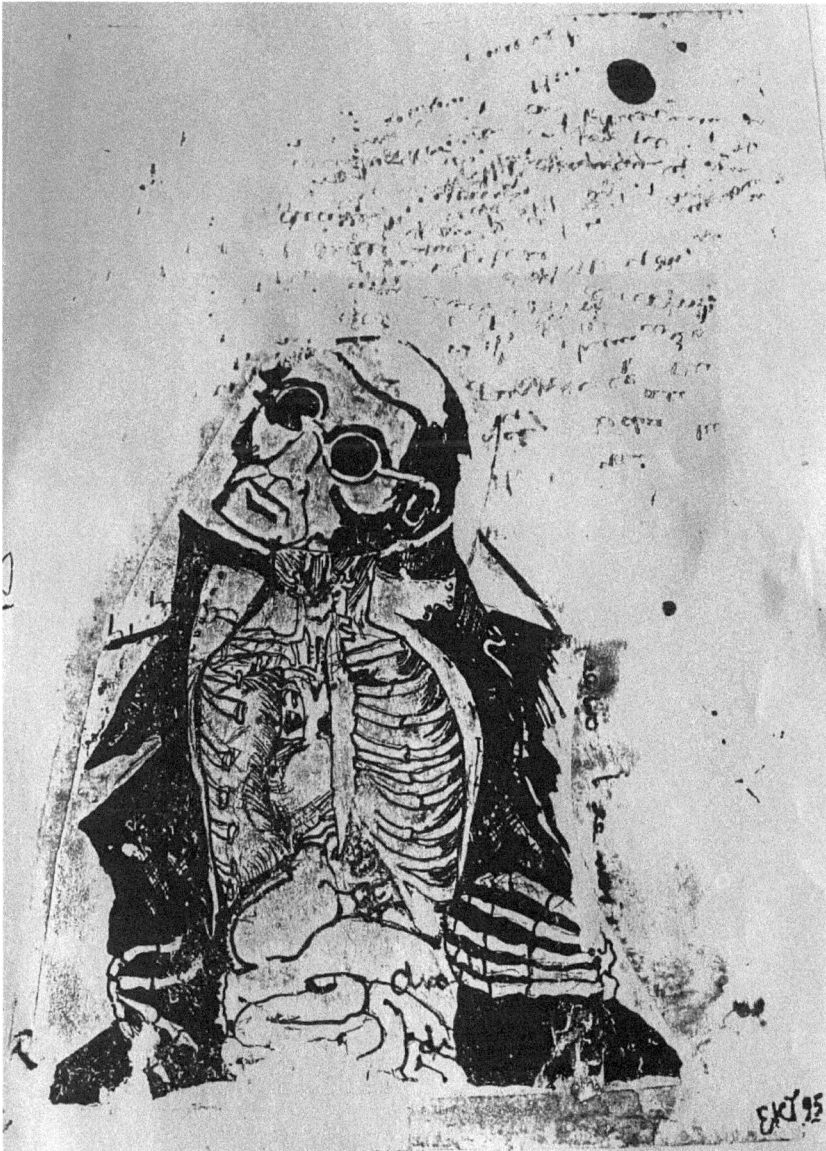

Characters

DAFT JAMIE	an idiot boy
BILL BURKE	an unrepentant murderer
WILLIAM HARE	a devious murderer
DOCTOR KNOX	an arrogant anatomist
An Inspector	
An Advocate	
A Judge	
Murder victims	

Commissioned by Clive Meachen and Douglas Houston, for Aberystwyth University's season of 'Verbals' productions. Performed at Aberystwyth Arts Centre, March 1992 with the following cast:

JAMIE	Charmian Savill
BURKE	Ian Staples
HARE	Bridget Keehan
KNOX	Louise Tickle
All others	Louise Tickle

Music by	Nick Taylor and Nick Jones
Directed by	David Ian Rabey

RESURRECTION MEN

JAMIE   Up the close and down the stair

There they go, it's Burke and Hare

With a body in a box

On their way to Doctor Knox

B/H/K   One, two, three, four

Bring the bodies to the door

Five, six, seven, eight

Get them fresh, but bring them late

JAMIE   The doctor's boys are on the case,

Pop a pillow on your face,

Give you whiskey, take your life,

Pack you neatly for the knife.

B/H/K   Nine, ten, a clear dozen,

Bare the bones, learn the lesson,

Four more makes sixteen,

Science is truth, trade clean

JAMIE   Up the close and down the stair

Round the house with Burke and Hare

Burke's the butcher, Hare the thief,

Knox the boy who buys the beef.

KNOX   The heart is a double organ – composed of two

hearts.

These two hearts are not placed apart, because

important advantages result from their union:

the action of their corresponding cavities being

precisely synchronous, their fibres mutually

intermixing contribute to their mutual support.

To see the interior, make a horizontal incision

through the anterior wall from the apex of the

unde nomen transversely across the cavity;

from there make another at right angles into

the superior *cava*. Observe.

JAMIE   Me then – Daft Jamie – killed

Not all there – bit here – ha ha goodun eh?

Here and there, here and there – goodun ha ha.

But here now, Jamie's here now – yes?

Poor Jamie's not.

Not really no, really elsewhere Jamie is.

Jamie's here but there and not so daft – really – now.

Maybe Daft is there, and Jamie here.

Maybe daft is bottled now, maybe in a jar –

Like his globes and peenee, like his nose and
heart – poor boy.
But still – by name Daft Jamie is and lived– the
times. See.
What, you need a picture
To conjure that squalor?
The teaming things
Born human beings
The rot and the rats
And the gurgling fats
Of the shit-swilled streets
And the skin in pleats
On the scabious frames
Deformed and lame
And the reek of piss
And the Devil's kiss
And God's low hiss
'That's life, is this'
Ah, you see it now:
And see there how
The crawling poor
– No hands but claw –
From a fair past Hell
Would gather to sell
Hair by the bale

Bones by the pail,

And what you see

Is what you get,

And it might be me:

And it's not dead yet.

Daft Jamie's daft

But Jamie's been

Where peculiar craft

Is practiced between

The upright citizen,

The downright denizen:

They pray for a nod

From the devil or god

Would trade a wife

For gravy and suet,

And that was life

As Jamie knew it.

See?

And see these,

See these nice gentlemen:

If you please

Three fine fellows:

They'll tell you

Hear!

HARE	Me name is William Hare, I don't care
	Me name is William Hare, best beware
	For there'll be a good ten pound
	To keep your corpse out of the ground
	Me and Burke, we don't shirk dirty work.
BURKE	Me name is Billy Burke damn your eyes
	They call me brazen Bill damn your eyes
	They call me brazen Bill and I damn you all to hell
	Me name is Billy Burke damn your eyes
KNOX	Though it seems I must speak in this crude rhyme,
	I will sing no crass folk ditty
	Nor present myself in lurid mime.
	I know nothing of this loathsome pair.
	I am a doctor and lecturer in anatomy:
	Robert Knox, number ten, surgeons square.
JAMIE	Nice gents, eh?
	Nice gentleman.
	Now
	Jamie told the times
	Didn't he?
	Told the times
	didn't have a clock

didn't have a watch

but Jamie told the times

Hee hee, a goodun eh?

Now -

To tell the trade,

Jamie's got another voice:

Jamie's got a paper voice, book voice, paper voice.

Here! Britain, the early part of the 19th century – the only subjects provided by law for dissection in anatomy classes were the bodies of executed criminals – the supply was never adequate. That the demand might be met – the robbing of graves became widespread – both by students, augmenting the supply for their schools, and by professionals, to whom it was a business.

To combat the trade – watch towers were built in churchyards, patrols instituted by relatives of the dead, iron mortsafes placed over new graves, patent locking coffins offered for sale.

Paper voice eh – what's got words and also serves, eh?

A page! eh? eh? Hah! Here's these gents again.

Here's Hare.

HARE   Here's Hare indeed.

Mister Hare to you:

A chap of particular creed.

In unfortunate times,

An unfortunate man.

But I know what I know

And dine as I can,

And do off carrion feed.

The face of a cretin, you say?

– Though not to the cretinous face.

Well now, my doves,

You could find

What's behind it is even more base.

JAMIE   Hairy stuff eh? hee hee, Hare-y stuff.

Here's Burke.

BURKE   In come I, Bill Burke:

So flogging what?

What's it flogging to you?

– You want to know me?

I'm Burke:

I've served militia

Worked the diggings

Peddled rags,

Sold skins, hair,

Cobbled shoes;

Now I've got new work:

19

Scientific, flogging right.
I've had a busted life,
Got a cowson wife,
I'm Burke, and you can flog off.

JAMIE   Sweet William, eh? Here's the dear Doctor:
In a class of his own, to a class of his own.

KNOX   In comes I then, gentlemen,
'Old Cyclops' my nickname, I believe,
Derived no doubt from my lack of
One organ of vision, a loss
Attributable to the visitation of
Smallpox whilst a child.
Gentlemen, be assured my
Remaining eye serves me
Admirably in the demonstration
Of anatomy, physiology and surgery.
I expect, gentlemen, your time under
My tutelage to be profitable to
You and have, to that end, secured
An ample supply of anatomical
Subjects for your study.

JAMIE	The charming MISTER Hare you've met,
	The amiable Billy Burke,
	The doctor their employer -
	No hear about their work.
HARE	There's a job that's done in the quietness
BURKE	Hard graft with pick and with spade
HARE	Plied in the grave's deep darkness
BURKE	A bloody queer, queer bloody trade
KNOX	Middleman, middleman,
	Cut out the middleman
JAMIE	Fiddle him, diddle him,
	Pleasantly fuddle him,
	Cut up the middleman,
	Less work and more song
BURKE	Black light and throat clagging sweetness
	That's earning the money you're paid
	Digging up this Mister Stiffness,
	Else hauling up that Mrs Shade

KNOX   Middleman, middleman,

            Cut out the middleman

JAMIE   Fiddle him, diddle him,

            Utterly cuddle him,

            Cut up the middleman,

            Less sweat and no pong

HARE   Why wait for natural illness?

            Why wait for the corpse to be laid?

            We're sack-em-up men and in business,

            Suppliers to the blade

KNOX   Middleman, middleman,

            Cut out the middleman

JAMIE   Fuddle him, muddle him,

            Most profitably peddle him,

            Cut up the middleman -

KNOX   If your blood be that strong.

            The nerves of the heart are derived from the

            pneumogastric and from the cervical ganglia

            of the sympathetic.

The nerves converge towards the posterior
part of the arch of the aorta.
Here they form a plexus called the grand cardio.
From this plexus the nerves proceed, in
company with the coronary arteries, to the heart.
But it is no easy matter to trace the nerves
into the substance of the heart.

BURKE   Hare, I'm flogged with it.
Plundering 'round in the stink,
Scratting for scraps worth tit,
Pressed for the price of a drink,
Up shit street estate,
Nice flogging fate

HARE   Billy boy, my darling man,
With nip in our veins
And a smidgin of brains
We'll put meat on the plate
And juice in the can,
We'll organise fate

BURKE   What are you on about, prickweed?

HARE   I'm on about dying Bill, dying

BURKE	Bollocks, I'm dying – dying for a drink, a feed

HARE	Bill my dove, it's others dying is going to sluice Your dainty gullet

BURKE	Flog off shite, I'm scratching at no more grave earth for running guts worth piss. I'm done with that

HARE	Dead, Billy, dead, you're talking of the dead; let them rot – it's the dying going to straighten us

BURKE	Christ's crud Hare, will you for flogging once talk flogging straight – who's dying? Who's dead? Who cares?

HARE	Billy Bill my precious germ, just listen: Here's how we'll make our empty purses glisten: No more mouldy corpses we'll be hawking Fresh meat Bill – we'll net them while they're walking. The passing trade that pays to lodge Within my house Bill, we'll royally entertain And when they're too far gone to fight or dodge We'll shut the air from lung and brain

BURKE   Twot

HARE   Smothered, Bill, smothered, they're clean and

               sound,

               Ripe for the knife, wrapped pound for pound

               And Bill, don't ask what the doctor will ask

               – Old manners and amputation –

               He'll ask not a thing, only bask

               In his lessons and reputation

BURKE   Gods rotten snot! You might just be a genius

               P'raps not all piss and puss.

JAMIE   Two men who felt the purses lean

               Hatched themselves a business plan

               For cheating graves without a shovel

               Sought grant from God – who wasn't keen

               Applied then to his famous rival:

               'Permission granted' – signed, the Devil

               Is that true, and is this false?

               One day, one will dance the waltz?

               Eh? Eh? Eh?

               Why is the last letter of HELL like people

               having fun eh?

Because they're both a party – part E. Goodun
eh, eh, hee hee.
Here's Jamie, here's his jests,
Here's the party, here's the guests

JAMIE   Joseph – a miller – last name unknown

OTHER   I was lodging at the house of Mister Hare by
               Tanners Close and in poor health

JAMIE   Soon to be poorer

OTHER   Feverish

JAMIE   Hare knows a reliever of fever – Burke

OTHER   Drink laden

BURKE   Here's the drop Joe, not of the best

HARE   Excuse me Joe, lying on your chest

BURKE   Excuse the pillow over your face

HARE   Give my respects to the better place

BURKE	Bye Joe
HARE	Bye Joe
JAMIE	Killed Mrs. Ostler – a washer woman
OTHER	I called by Tanners Close for gossip And use of a mangle
JAMIE	Killed Abigail Simpson – A seller of salt and camstone
OTHER	Just passing I was Going for my pension Eighteen pence and a can of broth
JAMIE	Killed A foreign man – name unknown
OTHER	Ja Danke - I haf drink
JAMIE	Killed Mary Haldane – a fat toothless prostitute

OTHER	Pelted by street urchins
	I took refuge in the stable
	By Tanners Close
JAMIE	Killed
	An Irish woman – with her dumb boy
OTHER	Me and the lad
	Was offered a bed
JAMIE	Killed
	Mary Docherty – a beggarwoman
OTHER	I thought – nice to be
	Invited to drink
	It being Halloween
JAMIE	Killed
	Mary Patterson – a young prostitute
OTHER	Slack eyed Hare – said I was
	'A model worthy of Phideas
	and the best Greek art'

JAMIE	Killed
	An old woman – name unknown
OTHER	Croak
JAMIE	Killed
	A drunk woman – name unknown
OTHER	Gurgle
JAMIE	Killed
	A woman – name unknown
OTHER	Sigh
JAMIE	Killed
	Old Effie – a cinder gatherer
OTHER	I'd got leather scraps
	to sell – tried Burke the cobbler
JAMIE	Killed
	Jamie Wilson – daft boy
OTHER	Gooooduuun

JAMIE	Ahh killed, poor Jamie, killed ohh
OTHER	Jamie Wilson – a daft boy – a character – well known
HARE	Here's Jamie, my dove, my chuck
BURKE	Here's ten quid with a bit of luck
JAMIE	Nice gentlemen – Why should you always show respect for a rabbit eh, eh?
BURKE	Twot
HARE	You tell us Jamie
JAMIE	'Cos it might be Mister Hare, eh? a goodun eh?
BURKE	Twot
HARE	Very good Jamie, very good – have a drink In return for your joke
BURKE	Yeah, get some down your neck – don't mind if you choke

OTHER	Jamie Wilson – a daft boy – three parts drunk
HARE	You look a little green young joker
	Could be drink or could be something worse
	Best let Burke feel your pulse
	Then we'll take you to the doctor
BURKE	'Goodun eh'? Toesnuff! Hare, you drop eyed pox
	Your jokes are worse than his clowns
	Let's get the little flogger down
	And in the flogging box
OTHER	Jamie Wilson – a daft boy – but strong
JAMIE	Jamie doesn't like this – not fun or game
	Jumping on a poor boy, daft and lame
HARE	Hell, Burke, the fool is strong, enfold him
	Get across his face – I can barely hold him
JAMIE	Poor Jamie doesn't like… he's wriggling for his breath, Jamie don't leave Jamie, don't go off with death

BURKE	God's shite, my balls, he's bit my bollocks Hare
	Grab the flogging pillow, plug his flogging air
HARE	Got it, got him, he's slowing, he's going
	Life of the party – nearly stopped him glowing
JAMIE	What's a coat you wear but once
	What's a coat that's wooden eh?
	You work it out ahh…it's…a…goodun
BURKE	Shite, the Doc will pay dear for his next specimen
	Blistered Christ, my balls are raw from this comedian
JAMIE	Jamie Wilson – a daft boy
	Killed.
KNOX	Much practice is required to make a good dissection of the face.
	The muscles of expression on numerous and complicated; they are interwoven with the subcutaneous tissue and closely united to the skin; their fibres are often pale and indistinct. The face is amply supplied with motor and

sensitive nerves, of which the ramifications extend far and wide.

Therefore you must not be discouraged, if in a first attempt you fail to make a satisfactory display of the parts examined.

Make the cheeks tense by filling the mouth with horse-hair and stitch the lips together.

JAMIE   Jamie killed – here – can talk

And there – even there – then

Nearly famous Jamie's nearly face

Could speak.

Here's an inspector.

OTHERS   Black Billy, Weird William

You are close to the mark

Should be taking more care

At your murderous lark

Should be taking more care

About who you death kiss

Should keep to the faceless

The ones seldom missed

Excuse us sir, Doctor

This subject's well known

It's Jamie the daft boy

Alive just ago

It's that daft Jamie boy

And he's here by a crime

For he's marked and he's warm

And he's dead before time

If Sergeant you're ready

And your men ready too

We'll take in this pair

And without more ado

We must take this pair in

'Cos it's said by some saint

That wealth care via health care

Is cause for complaint.

JAMIE   In dread time

To dead time

Unutterable dreams

Unsteppable dance

They are taken

In the blind hours

From amongst bones

And thin beer

They are taken

And go, muffled

Accompanying

The coatless ghosts

Jamie here – colouring it in

Usual blackness – usual blackness

All that – black heart black night

All that – usual blackness - black

More mauve, muscle grey eh? – that

Blackness – then this – near white

Eyes and their black specks –

Real black –that – Burke's

Famous eyes – that black

And

The body's caves

Lit in rose and violet

fluids of no colour

Somewhere a true pink tongue

Blood's Burgundy

Most green green dead green

And

Brown

Colour of rope and lies

Here's an Advocate:

OTHER   These matters are unclear

Is my submission

There are factors here

Considerations

For instance

Medicine and its advancement

The pursuit of science

Longevity's enhancement

Aspects of finance

For instance:

Expendability

Culpability

Liability

Probability

Admissibility

Also:

Morality, opinion

With their attendant mob

Demanding of this union

'The law must do its job'.

Well, if it must, it must:

Though in my view pragmatism

Here precedes that presumed just.

However, this apart, the evidence

Available is purely circumstantial

The prosecution testimony, insubstantial.

I propose therefore expedience

I propose to offer immunity

To that confrère in sin

Who first takes the opportunity

To save his own and sell the other's skin.

JAMIE   Round the town and in the gaol

Burke or Hare, who's for sale?

Hare or Burke, who will sing?

Who will talk and who will swing?

Who will walk and who take wing?

OTHER   William Burke will you speak against Hare?

BURKE   Me name is Billy Burke blast your soul

They call me Brazen Bill blast your soul

Me name is Brazen Bill stick it up

your lawyer's hole

Me name is Billy Burke blast your soul

OTHER   William Hare will you speak against Burke?

HARE	Me name is William Hare I've a flair for self-care
	Me name is William Hare and I'll share
	All I know of Billy's time,
	all there is of Billy's crimes
	I don't shirk lawyers' murk, dirty work

JAMIE	From where the world is slowing
	Where the dead live out their dying
	Jamie watches bodies file
	Sedate and upright to the trial,
	The bloody and the desiccated
	Nerves and organs separated
	Off to see their drama playing
	Some to weep some 'got to smile'
	Jamie says do this
	Keep it short – do that.
	Here's the Judge:

| OTHER | Who killed the Miller? |

| HARE | Burke plucked his power |
| | Turned his flour sour |

| BURKE | Worthless old swiller |
| | I plucked his power |

OTHER	Jamie Wilson as well?
HARE	Burke sealed his fate Shut and barred his gate
BURKE	May his teeth melt in Hell I sealed his fate
OTHER	The remaining fourteen?
HARE	By Billy every one Had their lifelines undone
BURKE	Done 'em quick and clean I done each one
OTHER	And what was the gain?
HARE	Near ten pound a shot Off the Doc for them hot
BURKE	For prime bottled brain It don't seem a lot
OTHER	Who will atone?

| HARE | Burke's fully grown |
| | Let his neck bone |

BURKE	I'm already flown
	Break my neck bone
	Burke stands alone

| OTHER | And Burke will atone |
| | With his neck bone |

JAMIE	Forwards and backwards
	What makes a lot of noise
	And breaks a lot of things?
	Backwards and forwards
	A bomb and a mob, eh? eh?
	Jamie's heard worse – here's Jamie
	Going a bomb
	Being a mob
	Hare killed and Burke slew
	But Knox paid and Knox knew
	Knox Knox noxious Knox
	Stretch Old Cyclops Demon Doc

Hare killed Burke slew

Knox paid and Knox knew

Knox Knox Knox - high high high

Knox Knox Knox – die die die

Hare killed Burke slew

Knox paid Knox knew

What does he want? A short rope

What does he want? A long drop

Hare killed and Burke slew

But Knox paid and Knox knew

Knox knew Knox knew Knox

KNEW

Old Cyclops turned a blind eye.

KNOX   Knox knew, Knox knew, knew what?

– to obtain a view of the retina the

Choroid coat must be removed while

Underwater, this is easily done with

The forceps and scissors – that students

Must learn, that Knox must teach – if

The choroid be washed in spirit the

Colour is entirely removed – that to
Convey instruction, subject cadavers
Are essential – in man this pigment
Is dark brown, in most animals jet
Black – That authority makes paltry
And absurd provision – the deep
Central spot of the retina is dependent
On an absence of colour so that the
Dark pigment becomes conspicuous –
That Resurrection Men do greater
Service to my classes than the
Council of the Royal Society – an
Appearance which is lost soon after
Death –

Knox knew. Knew nothing – of murder,
Knox knew this, that subjects taken
From the silent or the noisome grave
Were resurrected equally – from
Reeking death or dying breath –
All were raised and become part of
The matter of knowledge. Knox knew
And knows that learning shines
Sublime – all else flickers in the
Grime. Robert Knox, without regret

Quits time and, thankfully, this
Fatuous pantomime.

JAMIE   Ever the gentleman eh?
               Here's Will

HARE   Billikins my dove, dear hound
               Away to your long home
               The plank and the loam Bill
               The shallow ground.
               Death clothes become you.
               Tread steadily Bill, drop heartily
               Do the boots fit?
               You look so nice
               Billy foulmouth, sacrifice.
               Too brazen Bill by half Bill
               We were set for a career.
               The public like it quiet though
               You made it all too clear.

               Did you plait your rope yet?
               The clothes go back.
               Have the priests crowed?
               Fear is all you know of fear.
               Will you waltz it Billy dear?

43

Should have been more polite, Bill

You know I get upset.

Should've been more contrite, Bill

It's what the law expects.

The walk.

The knot.

The bandage.

The creed.

The bolt.

After your little ceremony

You're enrolled in Academy

Earmarked for anatomy.

That, Bill, is what's called irony.

Mister Hare's away

He's a business to resurrect

Elsewhere, any day.

JAMIE   A promising fellow eh?

             Here's Bill:

BURKE   You think you'll come up like a rose

             MISTER Hare of Tanners Close

             Well Mister Burke of Hang Street knows

             What's up your arse is up your nose

Hare you're a shiter, all mouth and maid's water

You think you know what's what – crap

I'm hanged Hare, I'm done and I'm gone and from

My side of the chopping block I see your map

Gardens don't enter into it, petal,

Here in Hell they've planned your path

Flint and ash and lickspittle.

Rosy future – don't make me laugh

Thrown into a lime pit for starters

Tramp and beg for a bit, poor eyeless gob,

Then they do a proper job:

Stoned to death like a flogging martyr

Eh, Sir Twot, Lord Snatch of Pissingpot,

Affiliate of the medical profession;

How do you like that true story? – not a lot,

How do you like that true confession?

All gen stuff from Hell's mouth though

Where we do have a vacancy

I'll see you soon you shitehawk

And that's called prophecy

I'm Burke throughout

And bow flogging out.

JAMIE   Lovely boy.

Lovely boys

Charmers everyone

Blind doctor

Corpse snatcher

Black butcher

What, you have a slight infection? (*mimicking Hare*)

The quick cure is dissection (*mimicking Burke*)

We'll get you to a specialist (*mimicking Hare*)

Your friendly mad anatomist (*mimicking Burke*)

Jamie says

Take a pill if you're ill

Says

What's a serious hole, eh?

A grave, hee goodun eh?

Says (*mimicking Knox*)

The tortuosity of the large arteries

Before they enter the brain

Is intended to mitigate the force

Of the heart's action

Says

The Doctor's gone, too indiscreet

Hare also you can delete

Burke found air beneath his feet

Jamie says – the tale's complete

And Jamie's ghost – is obsolete

END

'Alphabet, Delusion, Portent, Music': A Director's Reflections on *That Slidey Dark*

By David Ian Rabey

I was informed by the author that this startling and troubling play emanated from a trinity of mysterious kernels:

1. The traditional British folk song, 'Bedlam Boys': which may have informed or reflected Edgar's persona of 'Poor Tom' in Shakespeare's *King Lear*.
2. The revolutionary tradition of 'The Ranter': an unhallowed preacher, who might claim to be the vessel for the energies of both Christ and Anti-Christ; often insisting on an offensive essential kinship between the people that *Resurrection Men* identifies as 'the upright citizen and the downright denizen'.
3. The figure of the scarecrow, or mawkin.

In his book *The Scarecrow: Fact and Fable*, Peter Haining recounts three ways in which this latter figure has accrued mythic and ritualistic associations with sacrifices to nature:

1. An effigy at which people hurled sticks, perhaps in an adaptation of pagan rites in which originally a human being was 'done to death in this manner and then set up as an offering'; resonances which apparently survive in the traditions of Normandy and Brittany, where a life-sized effigy of Christ is set amidst the corn, possibly a Christian substitution for a pagan ritual of seasonally sacrificing a living being (Haining 1988: 57).
2. An idol who represented 'not merely an offering to the gods', but 'an image of the Deity himself, some Celtic Apollo, or Ceres, or Terminus', and as such may have been entitled to 'divine honours' (Maskell, quoted in Haining 1988: 58): a potentially terrifying figure, promoting fertility, whilst scaring off threats.
3. The mawkin: 'Apart from describing a scarecrow the word [also] can refer to the bundle of rags which bakers used for centuries to clean out their brick ovens before putting in the bread' (Lofts, quoted in Haining 1988: 58).

In *That Slidey Dark*, Wells's Whitey is a persistently unsettling presiding force, and confluence of all these associations: not least in his final resolution to cleanse these 'souls piping hot' by reconsigning them to the furnace 'spits'; or, to change the (somewhat Vulcan) metaphor, to the crucible in which he conducts his remorseless metaphysical experiments.

Again, the substance of the play suggested a performance style. I encouraged the performers to testify: to quarry the personal resonances of the text's words and dance them out; to let them Fly out with sensual pleasure, to be discovered, however surprisingly, in every thing. The text positively encourages the performers to work on implication, not on inference; as in Wells's other texts for performance, the use of (sometimes inverted) archetypes allow the performers working on and in them to be *peculiarly* personal. Our objectives in early rehearsals involve the imaginative and gestural construction of a landscape and a fictional odyssey for each character outside of the specific events of the play, as developed through circle-work improvisation to assist the performers in establishing free-associative dreamlike/nightmarish points of contact and play with (and between) their characters, in separation and interaction. These physicalized initiatives could then be selected and restored to imbue subsequent rehearsals and onstage performances with imaginative depth and force, both personally instigated and more widely mythic.

Scenographic designers Steve Mattison and Meri Wells became crucial members of the creative nexus for this project, as for the first productions of subsequent texts collected here. Steve and Meri characteristically and skilfully provided striking and evocative structures which the performers could use and play with in a variety of ways. Our performer of Whitey, Peter A. Groves, was partly cased or caged in an open metal structure, which also provided him with arm rests enabling him to maintain his cruciform posture for over an hour onstage. This structure was part of a larger design incorporating a "rake" of tree trunks which performers could stand astride, walk up and crawl between (Mattison remarked on how the splayed trunks also evoked a skeletal hand, and the bundle of sticks which often issues from a scarecrow's sleeve). Meri Wells noted (in conversation at the time of first production) how Nigel Wells's texts for performance are marked by the relative absence of conventional and literal staging, and normal dialogue and action, the continuance of which involves the literally demonstrative. Rather, this writing tends to 'open up, rather than close in' invention, by demanding that 'abstract ideas which are complete in themselves' – such as the line 'The forest is all weights' – are 'nevertheless located visually', possibly through something 'more akin to shadow play'. Meri's creative response involved developing, with Mattison, what she memorably described as 'pierced spaces': which appear more air than matter. These define the space (as positive and/or negative) by the point of puncture: so that the actions can be 'supported rather than enclosed' by a minimal structure. Correspondingly, Mattison and Meri Wells did not attempt to "light" the performers conventionally, but to create shadows which they could move into or out of, and so play with indefinition as much as with surprising definition. This extended to a questioning of perspectives, appropriately begging the question, where did the stage "set" end, and the audience(s) begin? In the auditorium stalls; or onstage, with Shift? Or with the musicians?

The musicians in question constituted an extended team, with a third multi-instrumentalist Peter Pavli joining Jones and Taylor, to form the expanded 'Brouhaha Orchestra': who added vital dimensions on many levels. Their basic instrumentation for this production evoked, but subverted, the associations of the string trio or quartet, mixing the more usually dominant notes of cellos and violins with guitars and fretless electric bass guitar, in a score which Nick Jones described (in conversation at the time of first production) as both 'very deliberate' in its evocations of chamber music and its points of interjection, and also 'very cheeky' in its changes of instruments and partly improvised elements. Jones professed to be consciously experimenting with 'sounds not so much disturbing in their associations as for their grating physical presence', and 'enjoying pushing aesthetic expectations towards the deliberately discordant and excessive'. The musicians were playing with, and consciously twisting, a style – chamber music – which they were aware of, but playfully unfamiliar with.

For performance, the musicians, Whitey and Shift were all established in their stage locations before the audience entered the auditorium. They were greeted with the musicians' introductory performance of an ironically genteel pastiche Mozart theme, and Shift's sardonic eye. With his rakish bowler, white gloves and loud check jacket, Russell Dean's incarnation of Shift evoked both carnival huckster and Master of Ceremonies, combining styles and movements which might recall Ian Dury and Tom Waits, with touches of Alexis Kanner's characterization of The Kid in Patrick McGoohan's television series *The Prisoner* (one reviewer also likened him to a figure from Stanley Kubrick's film of Anthony Burgess's *A Clockwork Orange*). Steve Mattison and Meri Wells's suspension of a chain harrow above the acting area developed the sense of juncture between the rural and the mechanical, as well as providing a shape through which to downlight and spill patterns of cellular chaos. The protean variety of lighting moods yielded by this essentially static object helped to establish the various locations, which Shift teasingly distinguishes in his commentary, through which the actions moved (as if in parody of the stations of the cross). This scenographic dynamism (connecting with Meri Wells's sense of the pertinence of shadowplay, and pierced spaces) also contributed to the impression that all things might disclose surprising facets, as if in a spirit of wilful trickery.

All the characters in *That Slidey Dark* seem to 'know more than [their] meaning' but prove vulnerable to surprise by self and others. For example, in her provocative alleycat sexuality Maudline is both innocent and disingenuous; but so are all the male characters, in their dreams of separative grandeur. Whitey's blanched garb reflected a traditional means to scare crows (perhaps his name may also evoke/invoke Clemence Dane's White Ben, 'God's Ben', as described and quoted by Haining 1988: 90-1). His figure stirred to life to rend Tom from his

51

'five sound senses' and rechristen him as Fly: Whitey miming the catching of an insect and placing it on Tom's tongue, as if in communion. Tom/Fly then froze on impact with 'the slamming entwine of the swarm' (on the line 'between the first touch'), while Shift led the audience in imagining a bending, writhing body, by indicating an empty space. Literal enactment here would diminish what the audience are challenged to engage with imaginatively: the incredible. Slightly behind Shift and his indicated void, Roger Owen as Fly slowly distended his face and body in a way which was figurative and emblematic of emotion, expressionistic rather than enactive. The swarm was suggested by The Brouhaha Orchestra scraping their violins, much as the stones flung at Maudline in the marketplace were represented by the thuds of discordant pizzicato. Calmed by Maudline on their encounter, Fly received her kiss as a further oral inspiration ('Draw in this breath'); on the line 'She dances him' the Orchestra provided a stumbling waltz for Maudline to school Fly in directed movement. After Fly's first tentative bids to develop an oratorical tone, his 'power voice', Maudline produced a mirror on her words 'stepping out'. Fly became further enthused by seeing the reflection of himself in full rant, and Maudline led him about the stage, as one might a donkey with a carrot, or a child with a reward. Her injunction 'Take heed' addressed the audience, and cued Fly's turning the action and delivery of his sermon out towards them. To approach the climax of this, Shift provided a chair for Fly to ascend into a single pink spotlight, and Maudline became overtly sexual in her role as handmaiden, assisting Fly to a state of mounting ecstasy which peaked on the line 'I am in judgement'. After this, he assumed a bizarre bathetic posture on the phrase 'I flap', which was reprised on its subsequent utterances.

Shift's song, 'Maudline and Tom', was a particularly exuberant set piece in our premiere production. Russell (as Shift) alternated between gruff and falsetto tones as he led the Orchestra through a discordant, Waitsian junkyard boogie-woogie. At the back of the stage, Roger Owen (as Fly) and Suzi Fowler (as Maudline) added a comic summary of events so far, performing a vamping Dionysiac mime of Maudline reeling Fly into a series of copulatory dance routines, summarizing their relationship in a comic, reductively bathetic way. Shift then concluded the song with an Elvis Presley burlesque, and Whitey became momentarily surprisingly animated on the line 'God only knows it's God's show', twisting his spread hands outward into a pose of pseudo-Jolson grinning showbiz razzmatazz.

   For Fly's procession (the sequence which begins 'Enter MAUDLINE as usher, FLY regally'), the Orchestra provided a kazoo fanfare, leading into a stately-sick violin theme. Fly appeared in crown, patchwork jacket and ludicrous fairy wings (also worn by Maudline), and Roger alternated expressions of ostentatious hubristic *pietas* with a lupine grin; then he ascended the splayed tree trunks to the highest point of the playing area, in order to exhort the audience to bow and 'flap'. Shift joined in Maudline's prayer, in parodic reverence, then in increasingly chuckling relish of its scatology. The assault on Whitey constituted a turning point. After the line 'Mad as arseholes', Shift suddenly became uncharacteristically bewildered, as he showed the audience that his habitually consulted prompter's script now held only blank pages and provided no basis for the increasingly extreme actions onstage. On the line 'I'm off', Shift left the stage, with an air of attempted dismissal, and walked out into the auditorium to take a seat amongst the audience (one of several excellent ideas instigated by Russell). Whitey moved out of cruciform posture and enclosure for the first time on his line 'Filling as it's emptying'; the end of his speech initiated a cello-led rondo, with guitar and violin, designed to echo his wrathful determination and continuing to underscore and reflect his power throughout the ensuing section. Fly's physical power waned visibly in Whitey's ascendance, with Peter's suddenly fierce delivery of Whitey's line, 'on my spits you're turning', effecting a particularly drastic twist of disintegration. Redesignating Fly's 'act' as a 'whim' (Whitey's own?), the wyrd mawkin removed the formerly implanted Fly from Tom's mouth (as if deactivating a golem) and crushed it, sending the would-be messiah into paralytic spasms of death. Maudline's desperate bid to rally and 'dance' Tom back into potency was accompanied by the sonic entropy of an increasingly fragmenting and splintering snatch of the previous waltz theme, which ended on Tom's collapse at the words 'Cast down'. Sensing her sudden isolation, Maudline obeyed Whitey's instructions, with a music cue suggesting her trance-like state. After a brief regretful glance back at Tom, and the shedding of her own wings, Maudline seemed to let herself be drawn into Whitey and incorporated into him, on his back, as her arms locked around his neck and her legs around his hips (their conjoined bodies thus forming a malign and inscrutable totem-monster, akin to that constituted by the menacing, assimilating Warped Justice in *Resurrection Men*). The stanza spoken jointly by Whitey and Maudline provided a false, or dummy, ending: a fade of stage lights and a discordant reprise of the initial Mozartian phrase. Shift's question, 'Is that it?', was delivered from amidst the audience. Shift then moved down onto the stage to dismiss the Orchestra ('Alright, lads') only to become suspicious, and then transfixed: the light faded, leaving his final rending cry in darkness. On lights up, the musicians returned to take a bow and pick up Shift's abandoned script; the performers of Shift, Whitey, Maudline and Fly remained frozen in tableau until all audience members had left the auditorium. The play-out music for the audience departure was 'Dem Bones' by Fred Waring and The Pennsylvanians.

That Slidey Dark is a precise yet ultimately mysterious play about strategy, manipulation, experimentation, and control: in short, the reaches of power. Appropriately, the rehearsal process was also mysterious, surprising, shifting and engrossing. At some moments, the characters seem to spin in their chosen solitudes like ostentatious dervishes, striving to hatch a birth or death from their own guts: at other moments, they seem like mechanical toys on the verge of running down, awaiting their custodian/owner (Shift? Whitey? Nigel Wells? Or someone – something – else?). As Russell Dean observed in rehearsal, the only thing that seems 'to keep the characters together is the words': more than usually

53

true here. Indeed, the characters often brandish the sound of their separateness (their own unshared things) at others; or else lock into the intoxicating spiral of a mutually confirming narcissism. No wonder that rehearsal improvisations often generated images of stretch and breakage, smiling and swallowing, weary disappointment and vicious frenzy. All the characters seem conscious of satanic exclusion, yet are subject to imbalance (awe, surprise, wonder) at the sheer extent of experience ('can they do that?'), which breeds moments of unpredictable engagement.

Prospective performers are advised to let the rhythms of the words emerge to strengthen the text's musicality and to combine with any orchestral score, and to listen hard for "springboards" which may generate cumulative effects and clashes (which should involve lots of fast changes in initiative, to startle, and so avoid any conventional drifts into melodramatic generalization). Avoid any impulse towards the ponderous and self-important: aim to be deft, mischievous, and appalling! As the original cast discovered, the strategic trope seems to be "to dance, initiate, and leave" – to express, seduce and then depart to begin a different action, and consign the witness to their own consequent demons. The springtrap ending also should work like 'the last kick of a food-processor that takes your finger off' (to use another Dean phrase) – as indeed should the endings of *Resurrection Men* and *Skin Shanty*. *That Slidey Dark* begs many questions: including, what if playing a role becomes more enveloping and vital than what generally passes for "real life"? A role is, at least, something. Or is it?

In rehearsal, we made up a "framework" context story: about an actor, SHIFT, who is invited to join his ex-lover in a production by her theatre company. She is playing the role of MAUDLINE, and her new lover the role of FLY, in rehearsal of a script given to her by a group of musicians. During one night's performance, as SHIFT watches, the actors begin to play out their roles beyond the guidelines of the script, until he is also enveloped. The musicians then reclaim their magical script and proceed: searching for another theatre company which it can devour…

THAT SLIDEY DARK

A Fable

CHARACTERS

WHITEY   A Mawkin
TOM/FLY   A Person / A Messiah
MAUDLINE   A Bedlamite
SHIFT   A Theatrical

Commissioned by Clive Meachen and Douglas Houston, for Aberystwyth University's season of 'Verbals' productions.

Performed at Chapter Arts Centre, Cardiff, on 22 January and at Theatr y Werin, Aberystwyth Arts Centre, on 23 January 1994, with the following cast.

WHITEY   Peter Groves
TOM/FLY   Roger Owen
MAUDLINE   Suzi Fowler
SHIFT   Russell Dean

Music   The Brouhaha Orchestra
                 (Nick Jones, Nick Taylor, Peter Pavli)

Design   Meri Wells and Steve Mattison

Director   David Ian Rabey

Costume Notes

WHITEY wears something raggy and enveloping, bearing resemblance to a surplice. From his arms dangle bell, book and candle. Around his neck hangs a pair of sheep shears.

TOM/FLY and MAUDLINE are raggy and medieval until they appear in their "Godskins" which are ludicrous and winged.

SHIFT should wear costume that sets him apart from the other three - a flash but shabby suit perhaps.

Musicians wear evening dress.

THAT SLIDEY DARK

SHIFT   A dark place, near a forest. Shift, an imitator and master of ceremonies, is shuffling, on the spot, a slow soft shoe. A mawkin, a little back and to one side, is a presence felt, then, after music, heard.

(WHITEY, in near darkness until now, is spotlighted)

WHITEY   From the hag and hungry goblin
That into rags would rend me
Spirit lit in a naked man
Bell and book defend me.

(bell rings)

SHIFT   Enter Tom, a pleasant fellow.

(TOM enters, humming, breaks into song)

TOM   I'll sing you a song, it's a very pretty one. . .

(his singing tails off as he becomes aware of tolling bell; he turns slowly towards WHITEY and is, at first, relieved.)

Oh hello old mummet, old mawkin, where did you come from eh, old Mr Whitesticks?
You had me going for a moment.
Oh just like the birdies on the wing
I thought you were a living thing.
But you ain't, you ain't, are you *(laughs)* eh, Whitey?
You flap your arm, you flap your sleeve
you're still old Mr Make-believe - eh - eh
(becomes unsettled) . . . make-believe - eh - eh
whats's here? what's ado? - what's - what's . . .

(WHITEY swings one arm forward, points at TOM who squirms and then, as WHITEY's arm locks onto him, TOM becomes mesmerised.)

WHITEY   That of your five sound senses
you now be reft, forsaken
so wander from yourself as FLY
'til mawkin you awaken

(WHITEY is returned to darkness. FLY, possessed, marches clumsily, incants)

FLY   Diptera: A large order of insects of which over forty thousand species have been classified - it is believed that these do not nearly represent all those in existence.
The flattened head is united to the body by a long and very flexible neck.
The divisions of the thorax are greatly fused.
The mouth parts are adapted for piercing or suction and often have a retractible proboscis.
The blow-fly differs from the ordinary fly in being of a greater size, having a light blue abdomen and in flying with a loud buzzing sound.
It is usually only the females which have sucking habits.

SHIFT   *(to audience)* Alright so far? Get the picture? Good, good. Now, as has been said *(glancing at script)*, "Oh do not mistreat the fly, he wrings his hands, he wrings his feet" - or is that brings?
Listen: *(music rises)*
A man enters a forest. He enters a forest with - so far as is known – no particular reason for doing so. So far as is known. He is no woodsman.
He is no charcoal burner. He is no gatherer of nuts, fungi, fruit. He has no professional reason for entering a forest. Or for that matter any vocational expectation. So far - as - is - known. He is a person entering a forest - its entertainments. With no particular reason for doing so.

60

Or for not. So - far - as is known.

The forest is all weights. It is made up entirely of weights.
Its components are all lumpen. How they press. From below.
From above. From the encirclement of between.
Probably - the - oppression - is - like - this possibly:

FLY   Clod, crud, curd, jag, wart - growth under growth over all.

SHIFT   Between

FLY   Slidey dark with chinks that hint at worse

SHIFT   Above

FLY   Boiled bedding pounding down is air.

SHIFT   As for noise. There is a sense of slop slop.
Though whether that is sound or feeling is uncertain.
There is also a faint but definite buzz.
About the buzz. Faint but definite, quiet but distinct,
 soft but certain.
Yes, well etcetera. Anyway it is none of these soon. In the
slop slop air the hard sounds slur.

FLY   Slurrzzz.

SHIFT   The first fly hits. Stiff-legged.

FLY   Between the first touch and the slamming entwine of the
swarm the cloud of the maze, life does not flash by.
Only panic - matched - to horror. Panic at horror to come.
One fragment of one second - for that. An instant? A flash?
A lightning dissolve? Such suddenness. Realisation that - this
will happen - that - before realisation - is happening.
Stretch this less than moment - to prepare - that . . .

SHIFT   He attempts to do something with his mouth.
His mouth's a cave for flies. Hoo. Hoo. Thoot. Thoop. He is
blowing. Hawking out the mass.
Trying. He is more frantic than they. He jigs.
He jerks, whip-cracks, snaps, flicks, flaps. Never has he moved so
many moving parts of him.
At once. At the same time. Joints, knuckles, muscles, flesh.
Everything of him that angles, bends or writhes he angles,
bends or writhes. He is trying to suck air - with lips shut
bubbling - farting through his nose.
His sphincter throbs - trying to close that gate.
They bung and forage - all his holes. Invade and take the stomach
bowels and lungs.
Can they do that? His thinking, touching that - begins to stray.
He must find other areas to get from this.
The centre of an awfulness - he is tightening into a deeper further
centre - to evade.
To escape the black froth that has him as its pulse
or eye or heart or seed.
He is finding - deeper than the raving black - the silent dark.
He is become -

FLY   a speck - at bay - at refuge

SHIFT   Mad.
As suddenly - they go.
What remains is - ragskin -
skinrag - skin and cloth, wretched, ragged - crawling
picking, gagging. The mouth - clotted still – burbles
and hymns.

FLY   All the little wings
little legs
little mouths
and their breath eradicate me.

SHIFT	Which is somewhere right. Me - has gone away - from skin and rotten cloth. Me - is taken by flies - is dispersed - become myriad - flown - buzzed off. Ragskin remains. Abandoned - being abandoned. Roots and snuffles, gouges all his vents - pokes out fly pulp. Clears that muck - but forest got in too. Something swarmed away and left him ragskin skinrag. So - outside washes in, washes out, washes in. There is now - nothing to relinquish, nothing to retain. Save the eyes still sing - a perfectly vacant thing.
FLY	Will fill though - must. Must harden - and reduce. Must make a way. That is the way. Floppy skin and clacking bones grope on. Curious locomotion. Drape and pile away - heave ho. Forest - and their seas - inhabit all - they suck and jab their way - to get their way - to be - interior. What chance for boneskin loosely heaped and open as a boat? I wipes and bundles on. No out, no in.
SHIFT	Essentially - spread. Only the eyes are meat - contain. Although – upon the skin a salt bloom tangles tiny hairs. Beneath this crowded skin are parcelled guts, crouching bone. It would seem an itch of death called here - crawled through sweltered rope, red juice - stuff like that - all to hug the heart, the pump and centre piece. Nag of death though, not its kick or clasp or arm. For now. Just - let you know - pave the way - turn the head. As it were. This spent sheet, in the vileness of time, furls to dream. These swimmy eyes - pearl to dream, flare, peel to circles, seethe.

(to audience) God - it's all work but, mad scenes,
they are hard going.
Still, press on. Music, my urchins, music.
(music, lights dim then spotlight on
WHITEY. FLY exits.)

WHITEY	I'll know mad merry Maudline
	I'll know what e'er betides her
	and she'll know love
	beneath or above
	the dirty earth that hides her.

SHIFT	A busy place, semblance of a market.
	Whitey in near dark - a presence felt.
	Enter Maudline - in pretence.

MAUDLINE	Dear ones, kind ones.
	Any pence, any drink or feeding?
	My mercifuls, I'll rightly take any you're not needing.

(to musicians and audience)
Here's a brave one, here a handsome,
and here *(to SHIFT)* a pretty, glinty - thing.

Beauties and baskets, all bound for caskets.

(Sung:) 'To find my boy of Bedlam
ten thousand years I'll travel
Mad Maudline goes on dirty toes
to save her shoes from gravel'.

Harlots and varlets, soon safe in caskets.

Sweet ladies
here one buxom, here a wand
sweetheart, girlchild, goodwife, scold
each modest, none bold -
tell Maudline, so she mend,
where to wander, where to fly
through hoop of flame and needle's eye?
to find a fool, to know his name.

Sweet ladies
(hand to head and then crotch)

64

here's sin and here's blame.
Kind ladies
any comforts, any food, any clothing
poor Maudline injures nothing.

(Sung:) 'And will I sing bonny boys, bonny mad boys
Bedlam boys are bonny
for they all go bare
and they live by the air
and they want no drink nor money'.

Oh sirs,
are not the witless wondrous
and all their foulness beauteous?
Here's hair would flay a back, sirs,
here's hair to strangle on
and eyelids sirs, and insteps
a belly deep and cool.
A nape to bare and a waist of air
the underbreast and the cuckoo's nest,
here's limbs to lap between, sirs,
here's skin to burrow in.

Oh sirs, don't ask
(hand to crotch and then face)
Here's a face and here a mask.

SHIFT   One gets the feeling the daft tart's not going
                 to go down too well with the locals.

MAUDLINE   Sweet ladies all
                 do not mistreat Mad Maudline
                 she injures nothing
                 she seeks her dear companion
                 although she's never seen him.
                 Spare a turnip, some meal, black onions;
                 your husbands dears - I'll wean them.

(She raises her arms to ward off missiles)

Not stones - poor Maudline cannot eat them
nor feed her fool your gobs of drool
when at last I greet him.

Hurt Maudline and be sorry.
She cuts mince pies
from children's thighs
and feeds them to the fairies.

My mercifuls, your charity
I've witless walked from heaven, sirs
danced in the dog stars gleaming
begged at the skirts of the world, sirs
and know more than my meaning.
Sweet ladies, Maudlin's a jester,
no harm in her, no harm
she injures nothing.
I injure nothing.

SHIFT   How to win friends yeah. Still six of one
half a dozen etcetera I suppose. Anyway . . .

(shifts from mocking to serious tone)

She moves, a traipsing, thin haunched creaturess

MAUDLINE   I tip my toes and drop my heels

SHIFT   from one place to another place and
another place and -

MAUDLINE   by beggary, by clouts and feels

SHIFT   fool's thought, afloat, ahead of her, leading.

MAUDLINE	To find my Flyboy far and away I do what I do, pay as I may And will 'til I find my brush-daft mankin Squat at his side, his bitch, his lambkin.
SHIFT	She moves, from desolation to desolation dragging her dullness and a tiny fire. *(To musicians)* Ah, play her away lads, play her away.
	(exit MAUDLINE. Music.)
SHIFT	A desolate place. Fly in flight. Maudline in rapture.
WHITEY	Deep cloud and the nether moon soul of whore, soul of loon, flood-wind and Hell weather bind them to forever
	(enter FLY, stumping up and down, engrossed in, and speaking to, self)
FLY	Life did not flash by didn't flash or even fucking creep by.
	(enter MAUDLINE)
MAUDLINE	Here's a flyboy boy if ever I saw . . .
FLY	Oh fucking no, oh no. . life like its fucking fuckmate death
MAUDLINE	if ever I heard . . .
FLY	sits, hangs or jumps up and fucking down on your back like a fucking big crate full of fuck all

MAUDLINE	if ever I heard . .

FLY
full of fucking nothing.
I'll tell you about life and fucking death
I'll let you in on the great fucking
idea of it, the fucking thing, I'll fucking tell you.
It's fucked - good - and - proper - Fly - has - fucked - it
good - and - proper. One Fly and only, to tell you -
the long and the fucking short - it's fucked.
The - fucking - fucker's - fucking fucked - and Fly's -
the fucker - who - fucked - it - hah!

SHIFT
He has a facility with language not granted to us all.

MAUDLINE
Here's my poor boy, Tom boy, Fly boy.

SHIFT
Best of luck to you darling.

FLY
(noticing MAUDLINE)
And who the fuck are you?
ahhh . . I fucking know you
I know you, fucking do too.

MAUDLINE
And course you do and so you do,
your Maudline come to brace you
Little lordkin – look
see you angels in these eyes
hear music as I'm speaking
smell you waves of paradise
between these gems a-breaking?

FLY
Fucking right . . . ohhh *(has sudden mood change)*

Yes, yes - I know you - must do - know it all now
everything - body - all - lot. Little wings, little wings
I was unprepared you know - but little wings - yes
I know you - little wings told me - wings came - know
all - know you - I was in a forest you know –

you do know do too don't you? –
I know you - I was in black froth
I got empty - got to be this - I was in dark - deep
deep - then quiet - I got to be this - know all -
this that - wings made me - ragskin - flyskin -
knowing - everything - skin. Know all. Know you.

SHIFT   Little Tommy shitskin
               Poor little sod
               Fell into a fly storm
               Came out - God?

               I think it's what he's starting to believe. Pathetic.

FLY   Know you

MAUDLINE   Know you.
               Long, long known you
               FLY's heel and heart
               His sight his heat.
               From a bedlam cell
               From the well of Hell
               Known you long, long.
               Watched for you, watched for you
               Spied on dear death for you
               Here now I'm wife for you
               Draw in this breath.

FLY   Know you

MAUDLINE   So you do and sure you do
               Know these ripe jewels
               This valley, these pools
               Know me and all and all.

FLY   Know fucking all

MAUDLINE   Tom's eyes were pearled

69

SHIFT	Not his tongue though
FLY	wings did that
MAUDLINE	And Fly was unfurled Knowing all
FLY	all
MAUDLINE	Into the world
FLY	world
MAUDLINE	To view the world. My bedlam boy, my visionary, I sing in Maudline gladness Bare and free what a world we'll see By the light of your sweet madness.
SHIFT	We will?
FLY	Will- will fill- tell -will tell - must- - heave ho knowing all - big idea - Fly's the fucker who fucked wings told - must make a way - that's the - this is - way - the way -little Tommy tree-mad - no out no in - boneskinFlygod - the mouth parts are adapted - will tell - am become - to prepare – Fly now - slurrrzz know all - know you -
SHIFT	Dear God, sort him out for all our sakes.
MAUDLINE	Dear God, draw in this breath. Here's Maudline will smooth you Her tongue on your tongue Unbruise you Lave you with spit 'til you glisten Calm you, arm you with Fly-words That world must needs listen.

70

SHIFT	And so she does pulls at his skin with her long mouth shakes at his neck and his poor cock and his wrists that are as insects are. And lovely spots of palest blood surface on him raised up by her her tiny fire - as alphabet delusion portent music.

(Music)

WHITEY	Sermons wild and winged Behind the tongue are swarming A pulse of fear, a voice as drear, Shall be the world's adorning.
SHIFT	I'll sing you a song it's a very pretty one . . . she attempts to do something with his mouth. she schools him.
MAUDLINE	My dear one
FLY	Slurrrzz - the mouth parts - will tell
MAUDLINE	Mine own - will tell - but, who hears now - who hears?
FLY	Eh? eh ?eh? all - all or none
MAUDLINE	says mine own, says mine own - and who bows?

71

FLY	all, under, everyone under the sun

MAUDLINE	to my lord, says my lord.

SHIFT	She dances him
	Turns his heels
	Turns his tongue
	Waltzes and reels
	Whirls him to words
	Gets him
	This hopping clod
	Going
	As it were.

MAUDLINE	Step we Flyly, Lord. Almightyness.

SHIFT	He's away, finding his power voice
	so to speak.

FLY	In the lipping of an eye
	At the sound, at the buzz, of God
	Was I changed
	My forces routed
	Utterly plagued
	Into nothing
	Enrapt in silence
	Where I lay
	Until all, all came
	Unto this, into this.
	Under terror and amazement have I been
	Poor Tom in the dark.
	But Fly has confounded darkness
	And come forth - brushed with whiting.

MAUDLINE	Says my Lord, stepping out.

FLY	Declare, declare Blood, plague, fire Sword, vengeance Declare, declare Overturn, overturn.
MAUDLINE	My Lord
SHIFT	Oh Gawd! He is, most mightily, away.
FLY	I am about my act, my strange act.
MAUDLINE	All ears shall tingle.
FLY	I am about my work, my strange work.
MAUDLINE	All souls shall tremble.
FLY	Flies boiled and broiled in Tom's innards Bitter, bitter wings in his guts; And they formed this true word The word I have and send forth Flying to all - with my heart - and all.
MAUDLINE	Says my Lord.
FLY	Filthy blind bastards call angels men Seeing no further than the forms of men.
MAUDLINE	Says my Angel.
FLY	Fly comes now - man shaped - but fully of the vengeance of Heaven - come to pour out the plagues of God upon the earth to torment its inhabitants.
MAUDLINE	Take heed.

FLY	I am come to make inquisition against all the blind holy, zealous, devout, righteous and religious who stink up the world. It is given to ne to expunge all that is admired, adored, idolised, magnified or set up. All that has been held honourable shall be brought into right and proper contempt - both persons and things. For this honour, nobility, gentility, propriety has without contradiction, fathered Hellish horrid pride, arrogance, haughtiness, murder, malice and impiety. I am about my work, my strange work - confounding all plaguey holiness and righteousness - confounding them with BASE things - every crumb of religion confounded by BASE things into nothing - and thereby, into -Majesty.
MAUDLINE	As poor Tom into my Lord.
FLY	Here's the mystery, here's the riddle - base thing so called, confound base things. When foul is as fair is - evil is as nothing.
MAUDLINE	Says my Lord.
FLY	It's given to me to speak great things and blasphemies for - to the pure all things are pure and what God has cleansed call not that unclean.
MAUDLINE	Cast down, cast down.
FLY	Take heed - you had rather hear an angel curse than a parson preach - a foul-mouthed oath from an Angel is more glorious than a slack lipped prayer.
SHIFT	Ho-effing-sannah I suppose.
MAUDLINE	Cast down, cast down.

FLY	Take head - as I plague pomp and greatness, likewise will I wealth - which is canker, the rust of which eats flesh with green fire.
MAUDLINE	My Lord shall apportion.
SHIFT	Mmm - a shilling for them . . .
MAUDLINE	Cast down, cast down.
FLY	Take heed - shitey holiness has counted lust transgression - yet beauty fathers lust.
SHIFT	Don't tell - mount up.
FLY	Base purity's confounded by base and wanton coupling my great instruction - fuck as you please, as you can - and for God.
SHIFT	Told you.
FLY	Here then's the word I throw.
MAUDLINE	Howl at the wonder.
FLY	True in my history true in the mystery.
MAUDLINE	Howl at the misery.
FLY	With foul and seemly appetite the most base in creation covered Tom and filled him and emptied him and filled him and so did confound him into eternal majesty, unspeakable glory, my life, my self.

MAUDLINE	Howl, howl.

FLY	I am in judgement.
	I curse, collect and lust
	by my right.
	By the holes in God
	I am about my strange act.
	Lord Fly in my Godskin.
	I suck on the wounds of God.
	I flap at you.

SHIFT	Yes, well, thank you vicar.
	A few psalms short of a prayer book this one
	don't you think? Course you do.
	Listen.

WHITEY	With a host of furious fancies
	To pull the world asunder
	And words thus tall
	Might Hell enthrall
	Sky-blest, sky-mad now wander.

SHIFT	They wander.
	Listen - I'll sing you a song oh it's not a pretty one . .
	(sings a jaunty blues)

Maudline and Tom, Maudline and Fly
come from above and below
Maudline and Tom, Maudline and Fly
God only knows how they go.

They tramp the old given ground
how they amaze and astound
populations and persuasions dumbfound
with their curious, spurious, furious sound
Maudline and Tom, Maudline and Fly
God only knows what they know.
They flap their wings that are fake

76

they howl - for God and fuck's sake
come one, come all now awake
to the clamour and the glamour and
the stammer we make.

Maudline and Tom, Maudline and Fly
gibber at the high and the low
Maudline and Tom, Maudline and Fly
jabber at the know and don't know
Maudline and Tom, Maudline and Fly
God only knows that, God only chose that
God only knows it's a show
old impresario, working on a tableau
God only knows it's God's show.

Phew!
(to musicians) Thank you penguins, well done.
(to audience) Now . . .

WHITEY   A spirit white as lightning
Now on their travels guide them
The sun to shake
And the pale moon quake
Whenever they espy them.

SHIFT   And so it goes.
They go on for a bit
God, do they go on -
until, one day as we say
they come to -
a different place.

WHITEY   A fool and a fool unholy
About their queer work queerly
Defend and pretend
At the wide world's end
What is, and is not, really.

77

SHIFT	Enter: Maudline as usher, Fly regally. They would have appeared to have sprouted wings. Hmm!
MAUDLINE	Bow down, bow down. Our Lord. Lord FLY in his Godskin, in his wings and wonderment - howl, howl at the mystery.
FLY	I flap at you, I fuck at you. I bring my lesson and most excellent way.
MAUDLINE	Howl
FLY	The magnification of curse. The abomination of coin. The consignification of cock and cunt.
MAUDLINE	Howl.
SHIFT	Yuk.
FLY	I am Lord Fly in my skin and my regality. I raise up, I cast down.
MAUDLINE	The rich, the righteous will he hurl into Hell. The foul, the worthless will he exalt. Fly in his Lordskin - bow down.
FLY	I flap. *(pauses - waiting for audience to bow down - they don't)* Flap.
SHIFT	I don't think they are going to play. Daft bloody duo - you may as well try and convert the bleeding scarecrow as them *(gesturing to audience)* *(MAUDLINE notices WHITEY and makes a slight movement towards him)*

Oh God, I do believe . . .
(shakes his head) . . . makes you weep.

MAUDLINE   *(approaches WHITEY)*
Bow down *(WHITEY makes no response)*
Howl, howl *(still no response - she turns and moves
towards Fly)*
Here's haughtiness in one, Lord,
uprightness that needs to be cleansed.
See. *(she gestures towards WHITEY)*

FLY   *(approaches WHITEY, circles him)*
I Flap at you *(WHITEY makes no response)*
Here is nasty arrogance *(notices and flicks at objects
on WHITEY's arms)*
and what cankerous wealth - Lord Fly
shall save you from green fire.

MAUDLINE   Give over, give over.

FLY   *(FLY removes the bell, book and candle –
discounting the shears as worthless - hangs them on
his own person)*
I flap at you *(WHITEY makes no response)*
Ah here's subtle, shameless pride must
Learn blushes and amazement.
Fly, in his skin and profundity, shall
Act for you.
Mr Upright-Oddsticks - I am vile and
I am merciful - I offer prayer.
(He raises his arms, mirroring WHITEY's stance)

MAUDLINE   *(between WHITEY and FLY in an attitude of prayer)*
As our Lord Fly has taught us
so we say:

(SHIFT also assumes an attitude of prayer. He recites MAUDLINE's prayer, a beat behind her, in muttering ironic parody.)

All boiled in a bowl were we
Made sick in the heart and the head
All tossed in the fat were we
And strung on the air by a thread

And oh must we jiggle and dance
Ever twitch in the fire and the life
Or Flyly rise at the chance
To turn no more on the knife

For little enough we be
And little the life we have led
When fuck all there is to feel or see
And less than fuck all to be said

FLY

Is our prayer
and - that this wilful stick
be brought to ignominy - which is glory
baseness - which is pinnacle
is also - our prayer.

I flap at you *(WHITEY makes no response)*
I flap at you
I fuck at you *(suddenly and violently FLY spins
WHITEY round and starts to bugger him)*

MAUDLINE

Suck at you *(MAUDLINE simultaneously begins to
fellate WHITEY. Music over these actions, which are
short, noisy and climax simultaneously. WHITEY is
unresponsive throughout.)*

SHIFT

Mmm, very earthy - I've heard of giving it stick
but never to a stick *(he chuckles)*

Never mind his wooden leg, whop it up his shitter.
Never mind his mingy peg, tap his mild and bitter.
(cackles) Mad as arseholes. I'm off *(exits)*

FLY   Thus are we delivered from possessions

MAUDLINE   which are rust.

FLY   Thus are you made wanton

MAUDLINE   which is blessed purity.

FLY   Thus are you honoured and cleansed

MAUDLINE   and become savoury.

FLY   Yet - none shall enter the company of Fly
lest profanity - which I count profound
pours fuckwise from the tongue.

MAUDLINE   God's gob unstopped.

FLY   Fly's ordinance:
By his piss and his blood shall you swear
By his seed and his wounds shall you curse
I command.

WHITEY   *(slowly swings an arm forward to point at FLY and
MAUDLINE, who freeze)*

Filling as it's emptying
Insides outside outsides in
This runs as though without a care
Yet fails to walk on earth or air.
Its brain's a cinder in its head
The heart all scorch-marked - brown from red
It falls to rise but rising falls
It has no balance left at all.

81

A mask with such a supple grin
On face that's frown from crown to chin.
And did I shape this manfully?
And shall I re-shape finally?

FLY   *(unfreezing, with effort and greatly unsettled)*
Eh, eh, what's ado, what's . . . what's? . . .

MAUDLINE   *(hissing and writhing - less intimidated than FLY)*
Bow down

WHITEY   This thing's of my construction
It does my purpose serve.
Senses swerved, a world unnerved,
These work my sweet destruction.

FLY   Command . . .

MAUDLINE   Howl

WHITEY   Poor Tom's longer Lord to me
I speak in sober sadness
For more dark visions do I see
Than Fly in all his madness

FLY   I command . . .

WHITEY   Poor Tom is Fly and mad - for me
I feed him all this fever
And what he is, he is for me
And is of me forever.

MAUDLINE   Howl, howl *(second howl is no longer command
but actual howl of despair and rage)*

FLY   Ah - I know you - fucking whitesticks - I flap at you – ah

WHITEY   Flap you may and fuck you say

82

Is all of Fly's great learning
But I begot souls piping hot
And on my spits you're turning.

MAUDLINE   *(howls again)*

WHITEY   Fly was ever my creation
             His madness I did fashion
             I who lit his garbled wit
             Sparked it with my passion.

FLY   *(pathetically)*
             I flap - I know - I have wings - I have - converts - power -
             I have - my right.
             Fucking Mr fucking make-believe - I was in you - bunged
             and foraged in you - my power - Fly's the fucker - I have
             my wings - my right - my act.

WHITEY   A whim was all your mission
             Fly-madness just a notion
             That Tom's eyes pearled his senses curled
             Might feed a darker vision

MAUDLINE   His Godskin dries - his feet clump
             Flyboy come, I'll lick you, dance you.

             *(She slides up him and attempts to lead him in a
             dance, he clod-hops briefly, then sinks with a moan
             to a splayed position. MAUDLINE reels back in
             beginnings of horror and disgust)*

             Cast down *(she hisses at him)*

WHITEY   All he did - to all, to me
             He did at my deep order
             All he said - in or out of his head
             All for my great murder.

83

MAUDLINE	Cast down
	Poor Maudline injures nothing
	What now?
	His Godskin's poorskin *(she strokes FLY)*
	(Sung:) 'Oh to find my boy of Bedlam
	Ten thousand years I've travelled
	Mad Maudline goes on dirty toes
	to save her shoes from gravel'.
	What now?
WHITEY	When short I've shorn Tom's feral stare
	And sheared his great apparel
	His wife of air as a skin I'll wear,
	So proceed with my long quarrel.
MAUDLINE	*(Sung:)* 'To save her shoes from gravel'.
	How now?
WHITEY	Tom's bitch, my creature
	Crouch upon this shoulder
	Shall be my itch, my darkest feature
	Ten thousand years the older.

(MAUDLINE's arms now move slowly forward and up from under WHITEY's. She makes a show of opening the shears hanging around his neck. She beckons FLY with both arms. He rises and moves towards her, head bowed. She unfastens his Godskin, which drops to the floor. She lifts his head and pushes it gently back. She encircles him and draws him onto the shears. He stiffens, she releases him, he staggers back and sinks to splayed knees, head falling forward. As it falls he speaks - speech stopping as head stops)

FLY	In existence - the flattened head - the ordinary Fly - only the female - a pretty one - a pleasant fellow – what's? - slurzzz.

WHITEY & MAUDLINE

So pick-a-back-wise will we go
Through light and darkness wending
And all and all their beginning know
But only I their ending.
*(As they speak MAUDLINE's arms slowly fall –
WHITEY's arms then fall but as they do MAUDLINE's
rise, sideways, taking their place –
MAUDLINE's arms are now WHITEY's.)*

(MUSIC)

SHIFT

(entering) Is that it then? - madness, rape,
murder, mayhem another jolly night out.
I sometimes wonder about trying a different line of work.
Anyway *(to musicians)*,
you can start packing up now lads –
back to reality. I'll chase up the actors.
(Moves towards them)
Come on girls, show's over *(he reaches down and
shakes FLY by the shoulder - as he does buzzing
music stars up. He glances at WHITEY
as one of WHITEY/MAUDLINE's arms swings
towards him. SHIFT feels himself becoming rigid and
struggles against it.)*

Eh - eh - what's here - what's ado - what's? - ahh -
(despairing wail)

Musician 1   A dark place

Musician 2   Near a forest.

Lights Out / The End

'Simultaneous Solitudes': A Director's Reflections on *Skin Shanty*

by David Ian Rabey

The tragic protagonist of *Skin Shanty*, Gerald Crowforth, is a man who claims legitimacy through appeal to the same tenets that reassured Knox, Burke and Hare in *Resurrection Men*: that 'science is truth', and that moreover it offers a means to the all-redeeming validation of 'trade'. However, Crowforth is also a would-be poet, with messianic ambitions, akin to Fly in *That Slidey Dark*; and, like Fly, Crowforth ambivalently resists that which would incorporate him; and he is troubled in his navigations by the anticipations of identity that love seems to promise.

Crowforth is Wells's fictional extrapolation and poeticization of the strange case of Donald Crowhurst, the yachtsman, inventor and would-be prophet, whose life events have featured in several documentaries and inspired other speculative fictions since the first staging of *Skin Shanty* in Swansea and Aberystywth in 1995 (these are summarized at https://en.wikipedia.org/wiki/Donald_Crowhurst#Movies_and_documentaries; the documentary which I would principally recommend is *Deep Water*, 2006; wider popular awareness may be informed by the films *Crowhurst*, 2017, and *The Mercy*, 2018). Depending upon interpretation, Crowhurst either ascends to a rapture, or succumbs to a delirium.

Like Crowhurst, Wells's Crowforth has staked everything he has on his chosen voyage, both materially and emotionally. He hazards all stability in a bid to overturn all reductive dismissals of his lifetime's efforts, and thus prove himself a man. This impulse is not without heroism, but Crowforth's terms of anticipation are significant: 'I have done something interesting – my system has noticed me'. Systems seek to organize data, to adjust the problematic, to reduce the complex, to accommodate only what its terms deem relevant: in short, to engage with a thing or person only in so far as it feeds the hunger for pattern which the system is constructing, and to avoid, reject, *abject* the rest. Poetry and tragedy (and comedy) expose and resist the limitations of systems. In *Skin Shanty*, Crowforth's hubristic and defiant faith in his system collides with another appeal to authority. He broaches an alien but primal network of claims to identity and worth, constituted by the community of sea-creatures. Unfortunately for all characters involved, the sea-creatures' appeal to definitive authority is also (like all such appeals) fundamentally systematic. Here, words become a strategy of avoidance and self-persuasion more often than a means of (self-)revelation: to tragic effects.

Skin Shanty consolidated the previous collaborators on staging these works by Nigel Wells – the author, Brouhaha, Steve Mattison, Meri Wells and myself – under a specific designation designed to reflect the equal input of many people: The Slang Tree theatre company. It also added a new recruit, Michael Bodenstein from Tel Aviv, who co-directed *Skin Shanty* alongside me. The scenographic centrepiece of the production was another construction by Mattison and Meri Wells: a structure - suggesting a yacht's hull, deck, mast, and twin ladders to its navigation lights - which was balanced so as to rock when subjected to sudden or more frenetic activity. On entering the auditorium, the audience immediately encountered the Crowforth performer (Paul Penlington, sitting in a pose suggesting Rodin's sculpture 'The Thinker') on his "boat", becalmed amidst dry ice and surrounded by the dim presences of the sea creatures. Moor ropes, which had garnered (genuine, freshly gathered and pungent) seaweed, extended from the mast into the "sea" of the surrounding black playing space. Visually, this provided another example of what Meri Wells terms a 'pierced space': a suggestive (rather than literal) image constituted by a relatively isolated thing that attempts to broach vaster indefiniteness. Although the ropes and hull suggested a more extensive mass below a notional surface, these were not stable: the deck would lurch, the lines tense and slacken, to counterpoint the performers' actions and speech, and Brouhaha's musical soundscape. The shiny white phosphorescence of the "boat" structure suggested a spectral quality, or bleached bones; its relative smallness within a predominant darkness served to enhance the sense of its isolation, precarity and fragility. Nick Jones's compositions and Brouhaha's soundscape provided, on this occasion, a pulsing organic-electronic soundscape: like Mattison and Meri Wells's lighting, its sudden extinguishings were rare, but therefore striking and profoundly suggestive.

To board the ship, the selkie Teresa-darlin' discarded her sealskin (represented by variegated fur and a pair of star-shaped sunglasses), revealing a rather childlike seaside playsuit. Hannah Baker brought mischievous agility to this role, somersaulting up through the rung of a ship's ladder onto the deck, with a synthesized music-box theme accompanying her assumption of the role of wide-eyed smiling 'dolly'. To "swim", Crowforth donned a lifeline (the end of which was tethered to the mast), jumped from the yacht, and rolled around the stage: Penlington's swimming motions and crawling movements deliberately suggested the ungainliness of one out of his native element. Teresa literally rocked the boat when she sensed herself and others out of their depths and hooked herself watchfully around the yacht's ladders to observe the entanglements.

Lisa Baverstock performed a *femme fatale*'s poise disintegrating into a genuine wish for self-reassurance, as she played Mary Kinney's encounter with Crowforth, an engagement which unsettled both characters' control to an uncharacteristic extent. After their moment of physical congress ('I flood'/'Absorb'), Baverstock's delivery of the line 'I am Mary Kinney and I only have to stretch my fingers out', shaded the profession of a characteristic power (at least, until now) with a wistful, sad awareness of former and future limitations. Mary Kinney's insistence to the exultant mariner, 'Still you are a Crowforth', reminded him of the boundaries of any possible transformation, with an almost bitter dejection. Their ensuing negotiation is painful and precise. Crowforth demonstrates a characteristic (and fatal) preference for generalization, whereas Mary Kinney is dislodged from her own previous ritual and habitual self-descriptions ('I am…'), repetitions and generalizations. She now demonstrates an agonized sense of particulars: that she is a '*deep* bride', a '*water* wife' offering '*sea* life' (my italics), who can only ever partly meet his landlocked existence and claims (Teresa also observes warily that the greed and need for transgressive contact occurs only 'Once in a while' and should and can only be countenanced in these brief terms). Mary even tries to disabuse Crowforth of his relentless idealization: when he demands a 'sweet sea-song', she tells him 'There are none'. By casting her as a supporting component in his own apotheosis, Crowforth fails to appreciate the natural existence and elemental function which she is prepared to try to forsake in surfacing with him.

In our production, Crowforth tethered Mary to him forcefully for his insistence on 'the knot'; then released her only to permit her to remove her hair (at this point, Lisa concealed her own long blond hair by ritualistically donning a bathing cap); after which, she gave him the attempted smile of a nervous undressed bride. Crowforth pounced on her with insensitive promptness and tied her to his mast in a proprietorial manner, as he extolled the material details of his own little world of the yacht. His enjoyment of power then extended to his tethering Teresa by the ankle to trail out of the ship upside down. His attempted appropriation of the sea creatures demonstrates his bid to assume control by ignoring any claims to meaningful difference ('I/we redesign system'). Crowforth combined elements of both genuine and disingenuous tenderness when he briefly released Mary Kinney ('Few probs OK'); but then, on the injunction 'adapt', he swung her aloft, obliging her to 'make do and mend' as a second component, tied at the wrist and suspended from the opposite side of the boat to Teresa.

The emergence of the character Mags darkens the scene further. Her punning, garbling, associative speech may recall for some the protagonist of Caryl Churchill's play *The Skriker* (1994), but Churchill's character draws nimbly on a wellspring of unseen events. Mags, on the other hand, awakens and pieces together her sense and plan by a slow itemization and experimental emotional colouring of the data she gradually perceives and unites. In our production, Sharon LeFevre compellingly performed this character as initially very still, then unfolding and building to active power. When Mags freed Mary Kinney and Teresa from their wire bonds, the sisters re-connected with each other like playful dolphins. As if interpreting Mags's presence as informing his own initiative to end his life, Crowforth slid from the deck into the momentary apparent calm of the sea. However, within a few seconds this apparent diminuendo was challenged by the sea-creatures appearing behind the yacht and crawling over it, like oceanic Eumenides. Crowforth's bid to design his own mortal ending was thwarted by the sea-creatures bearing down upon him with predatory stealth, then vengeful fury. On 'Ready or not', Teresa lassooed Crowforth with the lifeline and swung him around; May Kinney then used the line to reel him in to face the full pitch of her contempt for his treatment of her. The sea-creatures became increasingly intoxicated and frenzied, spinning and capering and plundering Crowforth's whiskey, treating their victim as the centrepiece of a vicious ritual game. Mags seized him as an unwitting and horrified partner in a forcible tango, then subjected him to an injurious chest-pumping action (in parody of applying artificial respiration) in which the others participated. The vicious "game" was then extended to the formation of a "ring o'roses" dance around their new sister 'Tes'. We decided that, rather than play 'Tes' as uncomprehending or infantile, the dazed Crowforth should begin to express through the tentative words of 'Tes' a dawning realization of what had been done to him, and a savage hurt. Thus, rather than suggest that the quelling and punishment represented closure, the actions seemed to open up awful new possibilities: how controllable might 'Tes' prove to be? Might s/he yet try to be revenged upon the whole pack of self-appointed vivisectionists? We also discovered extended resonances if Mary Kinney, in her last exchange with 'Tes', revealed a suggestion of personal regret of cruelty when confronting the consequences of her 'sisterly' actions, to the extent that her eye contact with 'Tes' on the line 'Here and here and here' proved untenable. This mood was effectively dispelled by Teresa's vicious teasing, which turned Crowforth's utterance 'Learning' into an awful, enraged screech – a 'learning' which Mags promptly attempts to limit and control. Finally, Mags and Crowforth sank downward, eyes and wills locked in defiance, and there was a blackout for the sequence of concurrent voices and Irish radio message, concluded by one final audible word from Crowforth: 'beauty'. Lights came up slowly on the yacht, a latter-day Marie Celeste enlivened only by the wink of its electronics. Houselights built to the play-out music, Marianne Faithfull's rendition of the Bob Dylan song, 'It's All Over Now, Baby Blue'.

Speaking personally, during rehearsals I was haunted by another song, its atmosphere and cadences, which I found informative in approaching the text: 'I Misunderstood' by Richard Thompson. Crowforth's strategic reflexes are unappealing but aptly identified symptoms of the "virtual reality" which informs and constitutes all too much present(ed) masculinity: the compulsive ironies, the deflective witticisms of displacement, the curiosity about others conducted only in terms of objectifying self-distanciation from them, the fear of engagement, the relief found in the (notional) security offered by electronic systems and cluttering material objects, intended to denote the man more manageably than any substantial, and therefore unsettling, interaction. Crowforth charts the ocean and "explores the world" as if to avoid exploring his self. However, for a performance of *Skin Shanty* to avoid a mere corrective of this posture and become tragedy, those involved might also be prepared to explore the following: Crowforth's naïve, stumbling attempts at a dignity (principally in his radio message soliloquy); Mary Kinney's surprise at her own unfamiliar emotional disarray, as she awakens to the loss and pain irrevocably caused by her participation in the communal female repression; the manipulative playfulness of Teresa, who plays the "dolly" in order to reduce others, with mock-pitiful excitement; whatever pain in Mags 'don't heal' and paradoxically makes her insist that she 'shan't feel' in order to reinforce her position as 'head miss': in other words, what drives the sisters' tribal-sexual reflexes. Prospective performers beware, here be monsters. *Skin Shanty* is a slippery, vengeful, recalcitrant beast to work with. It insists on its uniqueness as it excretes suspicion and separation, not only demonstrating the strategies for avoidance adopted by both sexes, but conceivably suggesting an ultimate irreconcileability of what men and women may want. This is at the heart of Crowforth's failed exchange with Mary Kinney, when the rapture of his heartfelt but simplistic romanticism seems (intentionally or otherwise) designed to block out any possibility for her to tell him that his feelings are imprecise and wide of the mark: even though her two-word reply tries to alert him to the fissures in his plethora, its lack of reciprocity. At the end of his book *The Paper Canoe*, Eugenio Barba writes:

> *There are simultaneous solitudes*
>
> *That will make us fall in love…* (Barba 1995: 172)

However, solitudes they are; and solitudes they must therefore, ultimately, remain.

SKIN SHANTY

A Voyage

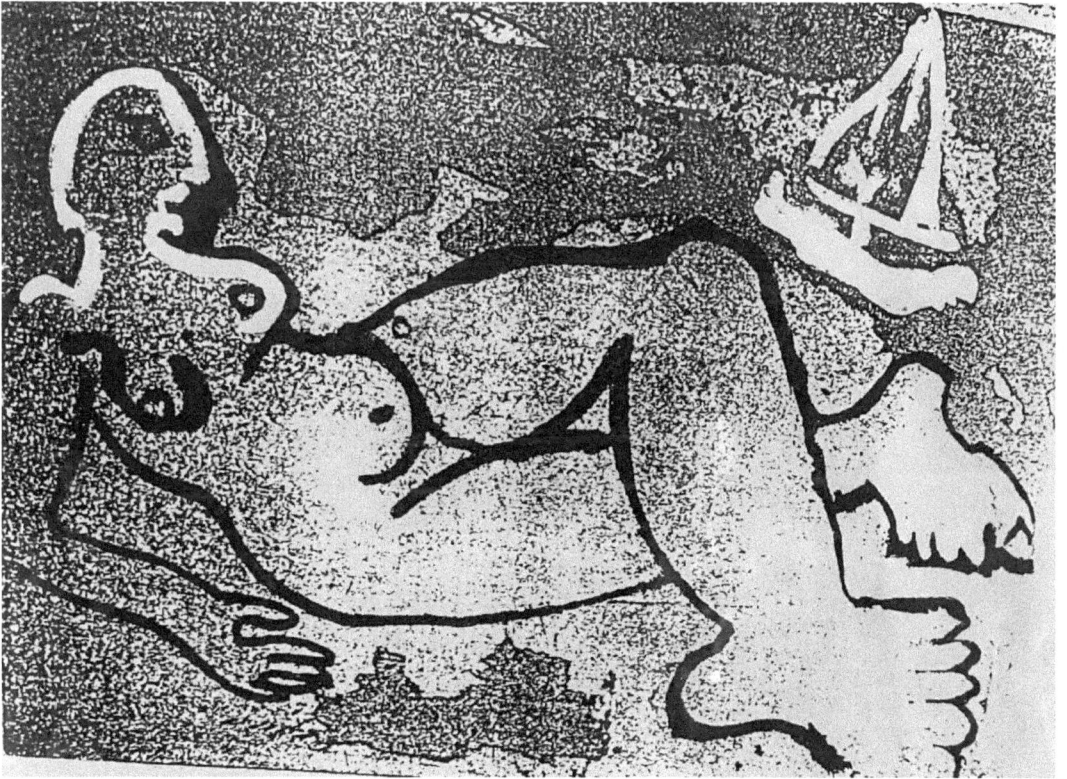

'*Mariners put your bones to bed*'
Edith Sitwell

'*... soon through my very skin
signals started streaming in ...*'
Paul Brady

CHARACTERS

CROWFORTH   a single-handed sailor

TERESA-DARLIN'   a playful sea creature

MARY KINNEY   a lovely sea creature

MAGS   an angry sea creature

Commissioned by Clive Meachen and Douglas Houston, for
Aberystwyth University's season of 'Verbals' productions.
Performed at Theatr y Werin, Aberystwyth Arts Centre, and at the
Dylan Thomas Theatre, Swansea, as part of the International Year of
Literature, May 1995, with the following cast:

CROWFORTH   Paul Penlington

TERESA-DARLIN'   Hannah Baker

MARY KINNEY   Lisa Baverstock

MAGS   Sharon LeFevre

Music   Brouhaha orchestra

                        (Nick Jones, Nick Taylor, Peter Pavli)

Design   Meri Wells and Steve Mattison

Stage Management   Sarah Barnfather

Direction   David Ian Rabey with Michael Bodenstein

NOTES

Crowforth's voices:

stiff-upper-lip braggart
troubled/deranged
parody 'sea-dog'
parody Irish
Tes

**

Musicians - semi concealed behind gauze - music should underscore
whole piece - be largely electronic with occasional flurries of fiddle
and accordion.

**

Stage should be the sea-bed. There should be the semblance of a yacht
allowing actors to be on board and to 'swim' down to sea-bed.

SKIN SHANTY

(Stage in dim green light. Voices off, singing.)

Lead	A little squeal, a little groan.
Chorus	Go down you blood red roses go down.
Lead	A little skin, a little bone.
Chorus	Go down you blood red roses go down.
Lead	Oh you pinks and posies.
Chorus	Go down you blood red roses go down.
Lead	Another push, another born.
Chorus	Go down you blood red roses go down.
Lead	A little fat, a little scrawn.
Chorus	Go down you blood red roses go down.
Lead	Oh you pinks and posies.
Chorus	Go down you blood red roses go down.
Lead	A little breath, a little taste.
Chorus	Go down you blood red roses go down.
Lead	A little love, a little waste.
Chorus	Go down you blood red roses go down.
Lead	Oh you pinks and posies go down.
Chorus	Go down you blood red roses go down.

Lead	My dearest dear she say to me.
Chorus	Go down you blood red roses go down.
Lead	My darlin' one you're bound for sea.
Chorus	Go down you blood red roses go down.
Lead	Oh you pinks and posies.
Chorus	Go down you blood red roses go down.
Lead	Oh there you sail and there you sink.
Chorus	Go down you blood red roses go down.
Lead	Your eyes can see, your eyes can blink.
Chorus	Go down you blood red roses go down.
Lead	Oh you pinks and posies.
Chorus	Go down you blood red roses go down.
Lead	Just one more and one more too.
Chorus	Go down you blood red roses go down.
Lead	All fall down the water blue.
Chorus	Go down you blood red roses go down.
Lead	Oh you pinks and posies.
Chorus	Go down you blood red roses go down.

(Stage lightens, CROWFORTH is aboard yacht bent over radio surrounded by chaotic electrical junk, and some wrapped Christmas presents. He is drinking from a bottle of Jamesons Irish Whiskey. TERESA-DARLIN is "swimming" around in the sea. MARY KINNEY in virtual darkness is sitting on a rock combing her hair - the rock or part of it is in fact MAGS but this is not yet known.)

TERESA	Swimming around - ready or not
CROWFORTH	This is Mike Whisky Uniform Tango
TERESA	ready or not, sailing around
CROWFORTH	Mike Whisky Uniform Tango on 12 megahertz
TERESA	Sailing around, ready or not.
CROWFORTH	Mike Whisky Uniform Tango are you receiving me, over
TERESA	Sailing around - once in a while I find one sailing around. There we are, here's one, here we are, ready or not.

CROWFORTH	*(Takes a drink.)* Try you again matey. Mike Whisky Uniform Tango calling, do you read me? Over.
TERESA	Ready or not.
CROWFORTH	Any station receiving - this is round the world yachtsman Gerald Crowforth aboard yacht Hydra of Erin, yacht Hydra of Erin, call sign Mike Whisky Uniform Tango - my position is… *(tinkers with radio)* my position is….
TERESA	Your position is - matey - is - sailing around and around - once in a while - I receive….
CROWFORTH	Do you read…
TERESA	I receive - Teresa-darlin' receives – in thingreen and surge - swimming around - in the deep - deep - in the shallow receiving.
CROWFORTH	My position…

TERESA	Your position - my position - receiving - Teresa-darlin' - seeing - poor one - poor boy - in the wastes of the water - poor thing, man thing.
CROWFORTH	This is…
TERESA	This is - me - one thing is me maybe is me girl fish funny thing - Teresa-darlin' in my seal thing fur skin - swimming around, watching for poor boys all alone - poor boys - he is…
CROWFORTH	This is Crowforth - sailing around. Aye maties if you read occasional spot of bother - good progress though - my position is - sailing around…
TERESA	I is - is in - own skin - my skin - lovely and deep-skin sea-skin in sea - ah darlin' in deep - Teresa in the drifts of the deeps - hugging and rolling her self-skin fur-skin - seal-thing - preening her maid hair, pale hair - leaning on wave air, rare air - watching for lost ones

- Teresa-darlin' - darlin' sea-bound, skin-bound watching for…

CROWFORTH   Ah then maties, here we are in the good ship Hydra of Erin - sailing around and my calendar watch tells me it is 11 minutes midnight on the 24th of December ie maties Christmas Eve and me alone on the not so jolly always ocean for two and a wee piece months don'cha know - oh aye

TERESA   All alone sailing around

CROWFORTH   All alone *(sings)* 'O little town of…' all alone with me little radio which don't want to play so, having already opened the Christmas bottle of Jolly Jameson, have another and open the packages packed by the old folk packed away at home for the skipper packed off to sea hee hee - a few bevvies a few pressies shipmates ah ha. *(He begins opening the presents.)*

102

TERESA	Swimming around, watching around - a foundering foundling- gifts he has gifts he has…

CROWFORTH	A silver spoon for my not so musty curry - a book of yoga exercises – shan't bother this side of Jolly Johnny chaps - oh no. Ah ha - a slab of cherry nougat nugget, just the stuff for the circumnavigator to get his teeth into - probably won't get 'em out till Easter, ho ho. And hmm! Looks like a dolly thing – ah well…

TERESA	*(excitedly)* ... he has… a doll - fairy fair - got it from his land-wife-girl - I spect he did - sure he did - ah a doll for speaking through - got a little dolly to talk to/through - dolly for a poor little being all alone boy. Ah Teresa's a dolly too - a darlin' dolly swimming around - Teresa's a dolly for the poor jolly boy - could be could be will she be she will be - surely she will - yes - but boy's on the float thing boat thing - so - Teresa-darlin' up out the sea - ah but can't in her thing-skin - not in her this-skin –

no hide that - hide it - slip it from the underskin *(lovingly she removes her skin)* slip it from the slip-skin - boy mustn't find it he might get the better - no - darlin' TERESA always the better TERESA-darlin' out of her top-skin hair dark hair skin into her plaited and pale hair fair skin - TERESA unwrapped…

CROWFORTH   Yo ho - Oh a clever young sailor named
Crowforth decided he just had to go forth
and sail round the world
so his sails he unfurled
and so and so on and so forth.

TERESA   … and voiceless - little dolly voiceless up out the sea - the poor jolly boys don't like our voice *(sadly)* little dolly's water voice hurts the jolly boys - put the voice with the skin *(she begins to remove her voice)* lovely, slippery water voice *(her words are disintegrating into breath sound)* put it tidy now Teresa dear and - voiceless, skinless, go lightly glide - up… *(She climbs/slithers aboard the boat while continuing to make breath sounds as CROWFORTH speaks. She pushes the doll overboard and takes its place.)*

CROWFORTH   So this poor little devil named Crowforth

sailed South and then East and then sailed North

but while beating back

on a Westerly tack

ran out of… of…hmm - brawn, brains and breath?

Huh - into gales, girls, birth?… rebirth…?

Oh bollicky bill me boys, stuff the old

philisophicles have a look at me last pressy

(TERESA is laying at CROWFORTH's feet still

making breathing sounds – CROWFORTH raises

her up and examines her) well stap me for a soak

of a circum a silly old circum circumnavigator - a

wee dolly… well, well - well and welcome lass

and a watery Christmas to ye - and me –

though tis the grandest of pities ye are not of stroke

in the flesh 'cos - ho ho

At night as the yacht Hydra lurges

I purges me sexual urges

with me hand on me pipe

I pipe up the band

'till a sticky white liquid emerges

oops - sorry no no listen now - will ye, will you

then speak wee one, will ye - no?

(he continues to examine her with interest and delight) - well doncha fret 'cos Cap'n Crowforth's at your service miss - I can sail the world, cook a curry, play the harmonica and ventriloq …ventr…ventriloquise - my voice at your command *(he takes another drink, sits TERESA down,arranges himself beside her as though operating a ventriloquist dummy - fixing lips, teeth, grin in ventriloquist manner)* –gawking, gawking - talking, talking…

CROWFORTH & TERESA

(in unison: CROWFORTH now speaking in sober voice – TERESA at first breathily but by the word 'crystal' her speech is automaton-like as CROWFORTH's philosophy is delivered through her) Talking talking to yourself - important, crystallise the thought, crystal set the thought – yourself – talking…ahh…

CROWFORTH   Feel tremendously fit…

TERESA   I am a lever…

CROWFORTH   nothing like the sea to get rid of the poisons…

TERESA	and my length and strength I determine…
CROWFORTH	few problems of course - but all part and parcel…
TERESA	my disposition and talent decide the fulcrum point…
CROWFORTH	nothing like the sea…
TERESA	my ideas the load…
CROWFORTH	in great shape…
TERESA	I apply the effort…
CROWFORTH	could play for England…
TERESA	and work miracles.
CROWFORTH	Few problems admittedly - becalmed for bloody ever in the bloody Atlantic on bloody Christmas Eve for one ho ho. Healthy though - never felt so…

TERESA   The stride of the mind.

CROWFORTH   … so…

TERESA   The knot.

CROWFORTH   *(fiddles with radio)* ... this is Mike Whisky
                (takes a drink) Johnny etc. …

TERESA   The great beauty of truth.

CROWFORTH   … never felt…

TERESA   To the stalled mind the present stage of
                man's development will always seem
                advanced. To the free mind the present stage
                will always seem elementary.

CROWFORTH   Uniform Tango - did I think you were
                listening old boys I would describe what I
                am doing and the actual hell of doing it.

TERESA   The free mind will, I feel, soon have access
                to the means of extra physical existence

making the need for physical existence superfluous.

CROWFORTH   Physically in fine fettle - light diet, the exercise required sailing the boat and, when sea is calm I swim - attached to a trailing warp - just to ensure I don't become a VERY lone yachtsman.

TERESA   To say this is to signal the process - to start up the process.

CROWFORTH   The hell - still nothing like the sea.

TERESA   I signal.

CROWFORTH   I sail.

TERESA   I transmit.

CROWFORTH   I swim.

TERESA   A natural phenomenon with a system of my own making.

CROWFORTH	few problems - no electrics, self steering unreliable, leaky hatches, faulty pumps, chafing sails, chronometer useless.
TERESA	My intelligence existing within that system.
CROWFORTH	Still one copes and continues - it is after all the nature of us sailor boys oh yes. Few problems though.
TERESA	I transmit…
CROWFORTH	I swim - yes clear the head - no bad thing a Christmas dip – no bad idea.
TERESA	… idea…

(CROWFORTH clips rope around his waist and goes over the side)
… signal…

(CROWFORTH no longer being beside her to ventriloquise, her voice now reverts to 'breath voice'.)

… transmit - aah poor boy's gone - swimming around - silly jolly boy gone out on the deeps out of depth - mind now, mind - mind Mags.
(she slithers to side of boat and watches CROWFORTH)
Teresa-darlin' has darlings, sisters dear - lovely and lovely but not so, not so darlin' dear as Teresa here, not so - ah swimmy boy

(she trails hands in the sea - playing with the water - pouring it from palm to palm)

- swimmy boy in the long low swell, in the grey-green, blue-green, weed-green, thin-green, long-deep, too-deep, sister-deep - swimmy boy in the swim so queer mind now you won't be a sea-tear - mind now - and mind sea-love and sea-fear - mind Mary Kinney - mind she might swim near - or Mags - oh yes, mind Mags.

CROWFORTH   Aah, and ain't this the liveliest way - swung on a long line - caught by three ply thread to a sea-speck, sea-house. Ah, tow me there.
Ahh me - little babbling valve on a bright bobbling sea, ah me.

TERESA   Foam boy flails in Northerly rinse - flounders in grey trader routes. Salt-doggy drinks - ducks from the life. Unfinned he slides - in wallowy trough - sluiced to the wide. Thingreen and surge, thingreen and surge - throughout his within - ah me - not yet - throughout his without - the sea on the skin in the beard.

CROWFORTH   Ahh, roll me in the rise and the fall - it is all, it is all…

TERESA   Ungilled he slides *(CROWFORTH sinks beneath the surface)*

CROWFORTH   … all, not all - ahh

(MARY KINNEY arises - she is poised, calm)

TERESA   Ahh… I…

(she fiddles with radio - there is feedback noise - she takes microphone and speaks through it while continuing to watch over side)
   … I transmit - and give you, poor piddling, paddling, puddling boy - give you Mary Kinney - who swims the ocean wide with her sea-scales and sea-hair that is the sea-tide.

CROWFORTH   (struggling for speech) You are - you - are…

MARY   You! What are you?

CROWFORTH   … are - Crowforth - few problems…

MARY   Crowforth! - and water-born?

CROWFORTH   … sailing around - swimming…

MARY   … that should build, that should burrow but roll in my billows and flail.

CROWFORTH   … swimming around - in deep - few probs – you - are?

MARY   Mary Kinney and I swim the ocean wide - and you are elsewhere and I am otherwise.

CROWFORTH   I am - you are - I need - in deep - few probs - bit of help -

MARY   You are - bodily - land mass in you - bulk of a boy and yet…

TERESA					There is jolly boy with his loss and his weight

						needs a golden lover, needs that green fate.

						There is MARY Kinney who swims

						the ocean wide and her gold hair

						is the green tide.

CROWFORTH				I am not easy in this water.

						I would be easy in this water.

						You are easy in this water.

						You are…

						You sea-scaled and gold

						you are still, in the fold

						of the sea while I flail.

						You are quite while I rail

						at the sea I would be easy in.

						You are sea-scaled and gold.

						I am not easy in this water -

						(looks up at TERESA - CROWFORTH and

						TERESA speak in unison - TERESA in

						ventriloquist voice)

CROWFORTH & TERESA - electrics gone - radio…

CROWFORTH				bit of help -

114

TERESA   Mind sea-love.

                *(CROWFORTH & MARY swim
                around each other)*

MARY   You are - bodily.

CROWFORTH   of help.

MARY   You are out-depthed - better and good.

CROWFORTH   I am a mechanic and a poet –
                a poor combination.

MARY   You separate.

CROWFORTH   Aye, I separate.

MARY   Your body stops you.

CROWFORTH   Yours seems the deepest water.

MARY   Mine is - through and through.

CROWFORTH   Mine is blockage and bones.

MARY	But in sea now in sea.
CROWFORTH	Bones.
MARY	Leave - leave bones - delve in the sea.
CROWFORTH	In the skin.
	(They examine each other's bones)
MARY	These are bones?
CROWFORTH	My structure.
MARY	What thumps beneath - this covering.
CROWFORTH	Blood - the pulse - is signaling..
TERESA	Transmit - da da daa, da da daa, da da daa, da da daa, da da daa.
MARY	Blood?
CROWFORTH	Liquid circuitry - I am an engineer and a philosopher - a dangerous combination.

MARY	No need - this blood - pulse - under the thick skin - empty that - here is thingreen and surge throughout all within.
	(They coil and undulate over and around each other - caressing with wonder and ecstasy)
CROWFORTH	Your thinskin - ahh - I delve – in your clearskin.
MARY	Blood-boy you are odd and beautiful - be water-wise - stay water-wise - I am Mary Kinney and I swim the ocean wide.
CROWFORTH	Was Crowforth but am losing myself - I am falling into you - dropping through your sea-skin - falling into love.
TERESA	da da daa - woe betide.
MARY	I am Mary Kinney.
CROWFORTH	The sea bleeds in my eyes.

MARY   My sea-shape in your eyes.

CROWFORTH   Once I was...

MARY   Delicacy of working hands.

CROWFORTH   My nails dissolve.

MARY   I am Mary Kinney and I swim your coarse hide
                plunge in your grit-skin and glide
                deep in your hair and your fear - here and
                here and here.

                (Touches his head, chest and genitals)

CROWFORTH   Ahh, - Mary Kinney - you reel me in - I
                writhe at your slim slimed breasts, nibble as
                a fish upon their long peaks, their slight
                fronds. Mary *mo chridh*, Mary my heart - I
                wallow in the age and ocean of you - roll
                and nuzzle at all creases and each mark.

MARY   Out of your element swim into me.

CROWFORTH   Out of my element - in my element.

MARY   Pour into my sea-wound.

CROWFORTH   Salt-wound.

MARY   Soft-wound, sweet-wound.

CROWFORTH   Dream-wound.

MARY   My rough man.

CROWFORTH   You dear sleekness.

MARY   Rasp at me.

CROWFORTH   Wrap me around.

MARY   I flood.

CROWFORTH   Absorb.

(They relax and are tender and loving)

MARY   I am Mary Kinney and I only have to drift my fingers out.

CROWFORTH   I may be Crowforth and I nurse upon your
                 belly and its throat.

                 (He does so)

MARY   I am deep sea - pearls and weed.

CROWFORTH   I was an electrician - here and now I feed.

MARY   Still you are - a Crowforth –
                 bloodbones packed in thickskinstill you are –
                 stop-skin - tethered.

CROWFORTH   Ahh, Mary Kinney - you say…

MARY   You were, you are.

CROWFORTH   Am? Mike Whisky Uniform Tango.

TERESA   daa daa, da daa daa, da da daa, daa daa da da.

CROWFORTH   Below and above - can role in love - can
                 solder, sail and rhyme - Mary Kinney won't
                 you surface with my bones - won't you rise
                 and shine and shine?

MARY   I am Mary Kinney - am your deep bride -
                        the sea moves through me - you move
                        through me - rise and rhyme through me.

CROWFORTH   Ah Mary sing me a sea-sweet, sweet sea-song.

MARY   There are none - you sing.

CROWFORTH   Mary Kinney…
                        Oh we shall know some journeys in our days
                        know moving silent on the ocean lays
                        know wave and dream upon our pleasant ways
                        and know by knowing what the water says

MARY   You misunderstand…

CROWFORTH   Oh we shall know brave voyages in our time
                        know tarry biscuit and a sucking lime
                        know ink and olive in our pretty mime
                        and know by learning how to work a rhyme
MARY   misunderstand.

CROWFORTH   And we shall know such journeys all the days
                        know salt and blood in coupled clay
                        know sun and moon, bathe in the shaping rays

and learn by learning how the body plays.

MARY   Bloodbones beauty boy you misunderstand –
                don't ask.

CROWFORTH   Mary Kinney will you rise - and bask.

TERESA   da da daa, da da daa, da da daa, da da daa, da
                da daa, mind now, mind love, mind Mags.

CROWFORTH   I am - this is Crowforth - thin seed - radio
                gone - bad yacht - dumb dolly…

TERESA   da da daa

CROWFORTH   … and you are Mary Kinney with your neat
                mouth - North and South *(he touches both)*
                and we must know brave voyages - you must.
                Here - the knot - make fast - my blood, my
                bones - surface with me - do. I will - we will
                - transmit - the Great Truth – the Beauty -
                Mary Kinney - rise.

MARY   I swim the ocean wide and my gold hair is
                the green tide.

122

CROWFORTH	Signal - the Great Beauty - rise.
MARY	I will dry.
CROWFORTH	No - you will shine.
MARY	Ahh - hard man.
CROWFORTH	Here - now - tie to my own tether *(he ties her)*
MARY	Dear man, dry man - you catch me - tangle me so - shall I rise?
CROWFORTH	Rise.
MARY	Ahh, but I am Mary Kinney and must leave behind - wind and hide my gold hair the green tide.
CROWFORTH	No need.
MARY	Yes - all need - sea sighs - all need - yes.
CROWFORTH	So well Mary Kinney - brave voyage - your head-skin at my silt-skin - surfacing.

TERESA   *(They slowly surface and climb aboard)*
                (drops microphone and slithers back to
                earlier position as limp doll)
                da da daa

CROWFORTH   Yacht Hydra of Erin –
                Mike Whisky Uniform Tango.
                Mary Kinney - the sea-house, the hub - the
                set - container of containers and all we do
                contain - transmit.

MARY   *(to herself)* Captain Bones - I do not contain
                - I am Mary Kinney and the sea is in me - all
                me - through - out.

CROWFORTH   So - here - your sea-home, float-home - oh
                what signals we shall send - not bad yacht
                really - fine ship - shall transmit, dear fish,
                heart's own. Here's radio - few probs -
                here's dolly.*(he takes up ventriloquist*
                position with Teresa) Back from my dip
                dolly - back from the deeps.

TERESA   Overboard.

124

CROWFORTH   And caught love - caught Mary Kinney –
             here's Mary Kinney.

TERESA   Gone overboard.

CROWFORTH   Oh we shall transmit signals…

MARY   Captain Blood

TERESA   Extra physical existence

CROWFORTH   and shall slip between - forth and back.

MARY   this air…

TERESA   within the system

CROWFORTH   Shall know the process

MARY   my hair. (*sinks to her knees and looks sadly over
             the side into the depths*)

TERESA   or systems

CROWFORTH   the process forth and back between the systems -

over and above and under - slip between - airs and

graces - between systems - I create - between

voices. Ahh - voices dilly dolly…

TERESA   intelligence system - human system -

CROWFORTH   … biological system - matter system… hear that

my little talk-drop - hear this - Captain

Crowforth's got ha hintegrated system now and

dolly dot's ha integral part -

(he rummages around amongst junk and pulls out

a long length of electrical cable - he ties one end

to TERESA - the other end has a jack plug which

plugs into the radio)

- got himself a clear tongue - whole tongue - got

himself a herself - got a dear heart - to transmit

maximum beam a good aerial essential - don't fail

good aerial - trail little tail - over you go.

Systematically - within the predicament - the

process ticks - away.

(He drops TERESA over the side)

TERESA   da da daa

CROWFORTH   She was only the morse tapper's daughter
                but she did it did it did it. Ho ho, ho ho.

TERESA   *(as she settles in water - suspended)*
                da da daa - Mags

CROWFORTH   *(turns to MARY)*
                See Mary Kinney - no more a dolly no - part of
                the radio - we are the radio.

                *(He flicks radio switches wildly - then lowers
                microphone over the side where it hangs
                suspended)*

MARY   My hair

CROWFORTH   Ah Mary Kinney - we are here. We were one and
                the other - bone against salt we were - thick blood
                on thin foam - sand skin on water skin - lone and
                alone - now we are this.

MARY   I miss my hair *(distractedly jabbing/combing her
                stumpy scalp)*

127

CROWFORTH   We were we - now this - connected we are
               the one – the great - component - in a blown
               box - yacht Hydra of Erin Mike Whisky
               Uniform Tango a transmitter - we transmit -
               in sea waves on air waves - transmit - the
               Great Beauty - the signal - we are - the
               signal.

MARY   I miss my hair.

CROWFORTH   *(going to her)*
               Mary Kinney you are my sea love. The
               female connector and the male - complete
               the circuit - confirm the signal. One land-
               locked one sea-free - merge - neutralise -
               form and confirm the signal.

MARY   Bone hard blood man - I miss my hair.

CROWFORTH   No need the hair tide Mary no need now -
               I/we re-design the system to accommodate
               hairlessness, tidelessness, endlessness.

MARY   Captain Love - I am not easy here - will not
               be easy here - light unfiltered burns me here

- I am clumsy here - my grace is gone. Your grace - below: my pretty fellow - here: porpoise mouth - bulge and bellow - below: all we are's familiar - here: dissimilar - our grace all gone. To be here - would need - as you - the pulse.

CROWFORTH   The signal Mary Kinney –
              the signal's now our pulse.

MARY   Wind waves - not true waves - you misunderstand - cannot be easy here - would need - as you - a muscle coat - bound on bone. My spirit splits - the sea goes past and under here - does not wash through - I am not slippery here - cannot be easy here - Captain Radio I miss my hair.

CROWFORTH   Ah Mary Kinney - you reel me in - I tangle you - we are the knot - we slip between. Listen - yacht Hydra of Erin Mike Whisky Uniform Tango - the transmitter - us - the components - ok - a few probs - ok but we can adapt the parts - to fit - transmit - it must transmit.

MARY   Captain Odd I am too dry to be here - too dry.

                        (she slumps - eyes open - trance-like)

CROWFORTH   Make do and mend Mary Kinney - adapt the

                        parts - radio - make it/us function - work.

                        Here - *(He pulls out another length of cable*

                        - it has bared wires at one end - he joins

                        these to a short length of cable attached to

                        radio – the other end he ties to Mary) we

                        connect - we slip between - establish a

                        circuit between - component parts - suspend

                        - in blood - in water -

                        (He lifts her up and puts her over the side -

                        she settles in water suspended)

                        complete the process - create the energy -

                        the signal - the Great Beauty.   *(He flicks*

                        switches and fiddles madly with radio)

                        Circuits joined, plates fixed in air solution,

                        sea solution - this is was will may be

                        Crowforth - listening stations - round the

                        world Crowforth - part and parcel - will -

                        transmission time to be confirmed –

transmit - the Beauty - transmit - signal – the
Beauty - all stations - any - receiving -

*(He rummages for pencil and logbook - sits and
writes maniacally)*

TERESA   da da daa, da da daa - no gold hair, no green tide.

MARY   *(coming out of trance and discovering she is tied)*
                No gold hair, no green tide.
                Captain Beauty binds me - winds me to his side.

TERESA   daa daa, da daa, daa da da, da da da.
                (whispers)
                Mags

MAGS   *(stirring, slithering on belly,
                feeling the water, keening)*
                O! O! O! O!
                hiss hiss what's this
                dead neap death knell
                rouse from rest - queerest
                bad dream bad smell
                no swift tide pell mell
                O! O! O! O!

in very nice skin scales dressed

the best but - tut tut

scales unstirred - sea

grows foul slows foul

sea glop sea curd

slow slop - breath - bowel

O! O!

Magskin gutters and gags

soupy stuff - salt glue

can't reach out can't see through

hate the hardly moving water

where's Mary Kinney - lovely daughter

what's sport her fought her wrought her

Teresa darlin' - what's caught her

O! O! O! O!

snort the stinch of manly bones

marrow wrack, bagskin stones

where's the pretty golden sister

where's the silly swimmy one

Mags smell Mags sniff - scent of mister

mister captain mister master

want my creepy ocean faster

faster faster faster.

O! O! O! O!

where is - hiss hiss - little miss - pretty miss -

hiss hiss - dead green dead blue –

this miss miss miss - one two mickle few - here this

queer miss - near this dear miss - bonny beeper

weedy weeper sister keeper

hooded sister stinchy mister sisterhood

deadwood bad mood should shall could can make

man merman – merman make maid - made maid -

Mags wade – did glide gold green hair tide –

who hide who's hide – sneak snide - open wide one

hide that hide his hide – his his – hiss hiss –

hiss piss - Mags piss – *(she urinates)* piss piss ahh.

(she notices while squatting the figures of MARY and TERESA)

Well now now well Noel saw three sailing by on
black latter day in mourning nasty picture runny
vista.
(She examines Mary - strokes her head - touching her causes radio to crackle and morse - CROWFORTH rushes to fiddle with it)

CROWFORTH   Yacht Hydra of Erin Hydra of Erin

MAGS   Was gold - brine gold - pretty Mary lovely
                              and glary shiny sister - see now sweet cow
                              no shine no glister - loveraboveher -
                              oh dear sea tear ahh.

                              *(She strokes TERESA's underskin - looks in
                              her mouth)*

CROWFORTH   This is Crowforth - all stations

MAGS   Baby bold everso old - slippery swim
                              singalongling - one way to skin a yacht -
                              yacht got your tongue then - sister darlin'
                              pester mister - bitter and good but - ahh.

CROWFORTH   Listening stations –
                              Mike Whisky Uniform Tango

MAGS   *(moving to, circling around and sniffing the
                              suspended microphone)*

                              Mags sniff Mags smell mister pester mister
                              lovely stinchy mister sister mister.

CROWFORTH   Do you receive

MAGS	Oh hiss - do Mags do - receive - receive mister – retrieve sister - Mags do.
CROWFORTH	This is Mike Whisky Uniform Tango - yacht Hydra of Erin - this is Crowforth with transmission - please identify - what station - over.
MAGS	Oh ha hiss hear this this is Mike Alpha Golf Sierra Mags-more-radio grim-green-ladyoh scalewearer seascarer sea station all station creation commotion ocean ocean listening listening
CROWFORTH	Identification recorded - timed at fourteen forty-two – please confirm you will relay my transmission to world stations - over.
MAGS	Confirmation given - riven.
CROWFORTH	Thank you listening station - important you do so vital transmission to follow - Mike Alpha Golf Sierra only station able to receive my signal - few problems with my transmitter.

MAGS	Say say current condition erudition transmission over and over.
CROWFORTH	This is Crowforth - yes - transmission now possible – utilizing combining components from Marconi Kestrel and Shannon Mark 3 with unit of my own design have created transmitter capable of signalling the Beauty. Precise relativity of own intelligence impulse with sea-trailed aerial of exact specification coupled with organic power source in salt suspension provide - for limited time period - the ability to transmit - the Great Beauty.
MAGS	Mister trans mister mitter advise wise commence immense mission trans as hands lands fourteen fifty four forty four - bystander - firm con.
CROWFORTH	Confirm - standing by.
MAGS	(goes to MARY - turns her full circle) Poor dear fair dear only hair root hair bare hair there there care for tide hair bride hair there there.

MARY	*(whispers)* Captain Barber failed me.
MAGS	Hiss hiss.
	(goes to TERESA - turns her full circle)
	Poor fettle wonder thing all only in an underskin can't singalongling - don't mind - Mags mind the tongueskin song-skin.
TERESA	*(whispers)* da da daa jolly matey trailed me.
MAGS	Captain da da sailed - did hiss did hiss - did it did it did it.
	(speaks into microphone)
	Make Wonky Unintelligible Tiny this is Mags Awful Grief Seawearer - are you receding? I smile - free fine foe from – I smell dry blood for English wetman - choppy?
CROWFORTH	Crowforth - Irish on me mother's side - listening station standby receive the Great

Beauty of Truth - message commences at fifteen fifty four and forty two - three - four.

MAGS   Spittle it out skippermayrue.
                        *(during CROWFORTH's message MAGS
                        sniffs out the hair, skin and voice and
                        replaces them on MARY and TERESA - she
                        hums throughout)*

CROWFORTH   Crowforth - once upon a different sort of
                        time - this is Crowforth - a boy was sailing
                        about - you will have trouble with some of
                        the things I have to say - Mike Whisky - had
                        trouble with them myself - Uniform Tango -
                        however set up basic equations saw the
                        pattern - now understand everything in
                        nature - in myself - this is Crowforth - in all
                        religions in politics in atheism in
                        agnosticism communism and systems - from
                        Julius Caesar to Mao Tse Tung a complete
                        set of answers to all problems
                        facing mankind - the poisons in your body -
                        you must get rid of them - I don't know
                        what they are but they've got to go —

the sea's the way to get rid of them - how to go at prophecy - nothing like the sea - the body is needed to carry the intelligence and to give mechanical reality to ideas and it has been the case that - the body stops the computer stops - our predicament - half body half intelligence - old system copes only with that - creation of own system allows for removal of intelligence - satisfactory - world stations - the sea cradles the life form carrying my intelligence -bound to Newtonian time my soul senses future freedom from the cradle - I introduce the idea of the square root of minus one - this leads directly to the dark tunnel of the space time continuum - emergence by technology from this tunnel will in a sense end the world - and provide access to extra physical existence - the mechanisms of second sight and prophecy - free will - the very center of the mystery - aspects I have no need to mention will tumble into place - an understanding of the driving forces will be reached - the system is shrieking out this message at the top of its voice why does no one listen I am listening - the system tells - but - formulators of morality unequipped with a mathematical dictionary do not understand the system language - mathematicians I appeal - this is the voice of natural truth - it is a loud clear voice and it speaks with the voice of correct abstract thinking - good souls flourish and contribute sanity to all intellects - enable the intellect to create better systems to contain actions - that has been my problem - this is how I solved the problem - I have done some thing interesting - my system has noticed me - at last - reason for system to minimise error - remove experience - many parallels - the sea's the place - seek truth wasting time - only elapsed time - sorry to waste time - barometer pressure on the move - time to move - physicality superfluous - my own making - time to leave - by my clock - Crowforth - Great Beauty - transmission continues - this is -

(He fiddles with radio - his signal is fading due to MAGS starting to release Mary and Teresa)

- is is is is is.

MAGS   Oh no ho hiss not on a little spittle life great matey of breath - that is it *(She disconnects MARY who*

slowly sits and examines her hair, breasts and 'wound') - is that it blabber mike
(She disconnects TERESA who moves and stretches, adjusting her skin, and protruding and examining her tongue)

it is that - give a miss - transmutant station - this is Mags Awkward Grapple Seanearer, now fall down the water blue - sweet ditty of death - time to - time to.
(MARY and TERESA now examine each other)

CROWFORTH   My message logged?

MAGS   Yes yes hiss wish mast dance girl fish mute trance hiss fish yes yes.

CROWFORTH   Few probs - components not ...

MAGS   No matter Captain Patter - time to - jump to - message where the mouth was - outreach - practice preach - fish wish - hiss.

CROWFORTH   Yes - understood.

MAGS	Stood under - under good - Captain Wonder - should -
CROWFORTH	Acknowledged - confirm time.
MAGS	Slip between - blue and seen - timed at - fifteen hundred presalty.
CROWFORTH	Crowforth counting.
MAGS	Tick tock the process - tick Tes Captainess.
CROWFORTH	Fourteen fifty nine and fifty four - the wade of the mind - and fifty six

(He unclips lifeline)

- the Great Beauty fifty eight - brave voyages nine - this is…

(he slips over the side - sits - legs apart, arms apart – head moving from side to side – whispers:)

Mike Whisky Uniform Tango

TERESA	Mike
MARY	Whisky
MAGS	Uniform
CROWFORTH	Tango
TERESA	Don't like Mike dolly don't - won't know Crowforth dolly won't - jolly Gerald - dolly won't.
MARY	In sea we drink sea - salt drunk we sip sea - roll in these billows drunk upon salt and in sea.
MAGS	In form who form uni form looney form change of take off reform uniform reform reform.
CROWFORTH	Tango.
TERESA	Don't like Mike - ready or not -

(She pulls microphone and lead from boat and ties tail end around CROWFORTH's neck - she swings him by the lead around her) dolly - not sound - once in a while we find one - swimming around - sinking around - once from a dial we wind one - swinging around - swinging around.
(She lets go of the lead - he spins towards MARY - who catches him and dances slowly with him)

MARY   I reel you in - Captain Whiskey - lapped at my sea-
                    milk, licked at my wound - ahh drunk
                    upon sea Captain Darling - drunk upon love -
                    drunk on the dance Captain Steps.

(They spin slowly apart - MARY to TERESA - who commence a slow dance - CROWFORTH slowly/dreamily to MAGS who, the instant they touch, leads him in a manic tango)

MAGS   Ho ho tango oh no phono seascape escape sea
                    party my party me hearty are you receiving -
                    reckoning recording recognising recollecting
                    recoiling re-creating reconciling remedying
                    recovering reclining

(She shoves him to the floor, kneels beside him,
pumps his chest)

respiring expiring - Mike Whisky Uniform Tango
May We Undo Thee Mike Alpha Golf Sierra
MAGS And Girls Souvenir -

(She pokes/prods him in various positions)
hiss hiss in form sisters un form mister hiss hiss
mister warm uniform hiss hiss sis sis.

(MARY and TERESA stop dancing - hold hands
and skip-dance, in manner of two school girls,
across to MAGS and CROWFORTH)

TERESA   Toy of a boy

MARY   Bulk of a boy

MAGS   Ahoy boy

TERESA, MAGS & MARY

          Thingreen and surge throughout his within
          Thingreen and surge unbone the skin

145

(They kneel over him - bone and emasculate him -
while singing)

TERESA   Another push another born

MARY/MAGS   Go down you blood red roses go down

MARY   A little skin a little bone

TERESA/MAGS   Go down you blood red roses go down

MAGS   Oh you pinks and posies

TERESA/MARY   Go down you blood red roses go down
                (Mags joins in on final 'go down')

TERESA   *(rising with several bones she moves a few feet*
                away, squats and ties bones crosswise into a doll -
                cradles it)
                Poor boy raw boy - poor Teresa - would be a
                darlin' dolly for any jolly boy - but the naughty
                folly boy put his dolly back - and Mags smacked
                the silly boy - whacked his billy boy – Teresa's not
                his dolly now - he's a dolly now - poor dear -lonely

dolly boney dolly - poor darlin' poor Teres poor boy poor doll poor boy.

(She continues to cradle-rock the "doll" - humming quietly)

MARY　　　　　*(rises - holding/examining CROWFORTH's genitals - she strings them on weed and hangs them around her neck)*

Odd body boy pretty man - I am Mary Kinney - would have been your deep bride - ahh - Captain Helpless sighed me - Captain Wireless dried me - and Mags slacked you boney boy - hacked your billy toy - pretty Mary sorry Mary - gold hair green tide - ahh - I am Mary Kinney and I wear what you lied.
(She moves to the rock and takes a mirror from it - she preens her hair and the genitals - humming quietly)

MAGS　　　　　*(crawls around CROWFORTH - examining him as she speaks - gradually she becomes captivated by him - by the idea of him as a baby sister)*

Well bell Captain Cock no phones no bones better
wetter better and good - bone less stone less - sea
in the skin - sea through skin in the swim - hiss -
with - in - through - out - ahh - oh sir sea merge oh
surge - sisters say poor boy pretty man - this sis
head miss don't heal shan't feel O! O! Captain
Babs in sea all fall all small all twirl all girl O! O!
mister mister - mister master - mister miss - mister
sister - master sis - miss sis *(she cradles him)* O!
O! what were – sir she - he her - sisters wrought
her - Mags nurse her - water daughter sister
daughter - mister fought her - MAGS caught her –
Captain's call sign *(pause)* Tes - Tango Echo
Sierra Tiny Extra Sister call her Tes little Tes yes -
best dress Tes -

(She scurries on all fours over to the rock,
rummages behind it - discarding weed, shells,
articles of flimsy clothing until she finds a weed
wig and a raggy/weedy blue dress which satisfy
her - she hisses and hums throughout - she scurries
back to

CROWFORTH via MARY and TERESA)

Sisters got a little sis Captain Baby Captainess
little Tes baby sis hiss hiss - come kiss this sis.

(TERESA and MARY hold hands and follow MAGS to CROWFORTH, swinging their clasped arms rhythmically – they are still sad but interested in the development. MAGS begins getting rid of CROWFORTH's clothing - blood soaked underpants are revealed but retained - TERESA and MARY dutifully join MAGS in fitting CROWFORTH with dress and wig - they rise - TERESA, MARY and MAGS assisting CROWFORTH - singing softly)

TERESA   A little breath a little taste

MARY/MAGS   Go down you blood red roses go down

MARY   A little love a little waste

TERESA/MAGS   Go down you blood red roses go down

MAGS   Oh you pinks and posies

TERESA/MARY   Go down you blood red roses go down

(MAGS joins in the final 'go down'. They turn in a circle, holding hands - CROWFORTH in the

centre - MAGS is thrilled at having a baby sister -
TERESA and MARY are regretful atthe loss of
CROWFORTH and his possibilities)

MAGS   Ring a ling a singalongling - goo thing plaything -
              Tes got a dress skin blue skin - not to mess.

MARY   Pretty baby - Captain Pockets was my posy -
              pearly baby rosey man.

TERESA   Tishoo tishoo down fall jolly fall once in a while
              blue fall all fall

              (They break the circle and swim individually back
              and forth and around CROWFORTH who, while
              remaining on one spot, tries out different swimming
              strokes)

MAGS   Tango Echo Sierra little Tes
              This Exceptional Swimmer.

CROWFORTH   *(from now on in TES voice)* Tarry biscuit…

MAGS   That Eversogood Sweetsy - goo girl slip and turtle
              slidey voyage aboard the Merry Mags no probs.

CROWFORTH   tarry biscuit pretty mime do

MARY   Baby voyager baby brave grow water wise
and we shall play at little boat and sail on
my billows - float our pleasant ways.

CROWFORTH   what the water says…

MARY   Wave and dream water babe - here and here
and here *(touching with both hands her hair,
breasts and 'wound')* - wave and dream slip
between.

CROWFORTH   the body plays…

TERESA   Playing around - poor thing - ready or not -
lost its da da - lost in the has been she green.

CROWFORTH   learning how to rhyme…

TERESA   Little darlin' lost thing when you grow we
go - rhyming and rolling around - swimming
around.

CROWFORTH   learning…

(MAGS possessively takes hold of CROWFORTH and prances in play with him - TERESA and MARY lean on each other and watch)

MAGS

Mags learn you turn you bonny nipper pretty kipper very nice Mags mams tickle sis teach you tuck you.

CROWFORTH

beautiful cradle…

MAGS

Full beauty ooh got goo Tes skin new skin blue skin ooh   flapper snapper Mags lead weed feed ooh.

CROWFORTH

tarry biscuit.

MAGS

Ahh - Tes blue - time to.

(lights cut to darkness - all four speak in unison and end together, except CROWFORTH's last word 'Beauty' which overruns and is isolated)

MAGS Mags hiss Atlantic frantic ocean commotion Must All Go Seaward Mams Always Get Seasis Mags-more-radio Might Arrange Grief Sisters Mags bags babs hiss.

MARY I am Mary Kinney and I swim the ocean wide and my gold hair is the green tide oh my dear man my dear wound you dried.

TERESA Teresa darlin' swimming around - found a long thing in a wrong skin - wish he find a song skin - fell into a miss skin - poor jolly boy.

CROWFORTH *(singing in CROWFORTH voice)*
We three Kings of Orient are *(speaking in CROWFORTH voice)*
you receiving me this is Crowforth on 12 megaherts moving silent *(speaking in TES voice)*
sucking lime - all the days - water says - *(speaking in CROWFORTH voice)* Beauty.

(A moment's silence; then radio starts to crackle and flash – it can be seen the stage is now empty - the radio speaks - an Irish female voice)

RADIO   Hello there - this is yacht Hydra of Erin –

Hydra of Erin

Mike Whisky Uniform Tango Tango da da daa

Hydra of Erin da da Erin

Echo Romeo India November

Echo Romeo November

Echo Romeo Romeo

Echo Romeo

Echo echo echo echo echo echo

(This fades into Morse code)

END

Wordskill: *The Glory Reel,* and beyond…

by David Ian Rabey

1. *The Glory Reel*: pain to stop the pain

The final text in this volume reunited Nigel Wells with Brouhaha (Jones, Pavli and Taylor) and the scenographic team of Steve Mattison and Meri Wells. Wells also featured as a performer (playing the acerbic spirit guide, Caller) alongside Will Kaufman and Sister P, and the performance was directed by Michael Bodenstein. I attended the performance, but I was not involved in this rehearsal and production process, hence the relative brevity of these observations.

The Glory Reel pitches two characters, Player and Dancer, into a dreamlike waystation of an afterlife, a limbo or purgatory, where Caller – a spirit appointed to orient and 'resettle' them – reluctantly presides, as the offhand and disrespectful emissary of a (feminine) deity. Caller interprets his latest allocated form, that of an owl, to be an insulting ignominy, when he maintains it is widely known that he prefers 'scales' to 'feathers'. Nevertheless, he wryly proceeds in the process of disencumbering the two new arrivals from their lifetime identities and assumptions, conducting them through a stage where 'memory and armament are forfeit', when guided towards the 'place you are not now nor ever will be'.

Thus, the basic premise of *The Glory Reel* may recall other dramatic imaginings of afterlife and/or (possible) purgatory, such as Jean-Paul Sartre's *Huis Clos* (1944) and Samuel Beckett's *Play* (1963) and (perhaps) *Waiting for Godot* (1952). The role of the idiosyncratic reception guide may remind some of the function of The Conductor in Michael Powell and Emeric Pressburger's *A Matter of Life and Death* (1946) (more personally, Dancer's situation as a Western cowboy consigned to an apparently posthumous ordeal to question his proud unkindness reminds me of the 1974 Pete Atkin and Clive James song, 'Tenderfoot'). The unsettling experience of suspended will and consequence, where characters and matters intrinsically do not and cannot "move on" except through delay and subsequently deepened self-reflection, also makes for difficulties in sudden or startling dramatic (inter)action: Player seems wryly self-aware of their newly discovered (self-?)restrictions when she tells Dancer 'a poem's not conversation'. However, *The Glory Reel* is vitalized by some of Wells's best writing, in the metrical interjections which received choric musical settings, and which approach the ultimate imaginative challenge: the intrinsically human levelling prospect of inevitable death. This focusses most pungently on decay and abandonment, how the erotic slides into the entropic, the loss of defence against the inevitable steady 'queue' – or startling headlong fall – to dissolution: the enforced relinquishment of claims to selfhood, senses, and memory.

Indeed, the two representatives of humanity, Player and Dancer, have formerly characterised themselves principally through their unusually heretically refined dedications to: smell and taste, nose and tongue (Player); sight and hearing, eye and ear (Dancer). Player may seem a development of Maudline in *That Slidey Dark*, in her bid to embrace what is usually designated abject with a fervour and savour which would collapse traditional boundaries in a bid for a transcendental 'serene gratification found in the living body'. She professes a religious dedication to approaching the apotheosis of flesh when 'tangible language rears through the pores'. It is another grim joke that her bid to worship through channels which might be associated with desecration has ended with her forcible and fatal confinement to a latrine.

Dancer's carefully constructed armour of rhetoric and manner, that of the laconic lone-wolf Western outlaw, flatters his career as a cannibal butcher of both guilty and innocent. His list of achievements, as itemised by Caller, suggest that he is not so much of a figure from a John Wayne or Clint Eastwood film, but rather closer to the consciously appalling characters we find in Cormac McCarthy's *Blood Meridian* (1985), or even *Child of God* (1973). Whereas Player generally navigates by a cheerful and accommodating discourse built on phatic communion, Dancer withdraws, even as he professes hunger to find his own chosen time and terms to say 'his piece': an ultimately deterministic cycle of masculinity which rages at its own restrictions and finds its kernel in the resonantly unanswered question: 'is pain the only thing to ease the pain'. Like Fly in *That Slidey Dark*, he seems determined to expunge what has traditionally been idealized, confound what is elevated. However, Dancer seems to have been less focussed on casting down pomp, vanity and wealth, more grimly malicious to a separative, severing and ultimately self-defeating extent. Player argues that her life has, contrastingly, been one of worship, not desecration. When she proves undamaged by his violent denial that he might (even latently to himself) be a 'queer dear', their opposition is resolved into an embrace, though the stage directions specify that they hug '*in comfort rather than passion*'.

In *The Glory Reel*, the whimsical and mischievous female deity remains resolutely unseen, not present and directive as was (the nonetheless mysterious) Whitey in *That Slidey Dark*. Caller claims to be pleasantly surprised by how quickly he can provoke Player and Dancer into realization of their situation, perhaps most decisively reached when Player puts Dancer into the past tense with the simple words, 'So you were'. Then Caller himself is enveloped in the action and process, despite his bid to maintain (self-defensive?) ironic commentary (a fate paralleling that of Shift): his appointment is the next for the forfeit and shattering of form, and attachment to forms. Notably in production, his dismissively irreverent bravado at exit was succeeded by sounds which suggested some degree of festive relief, even a brief shared and literally dissolute revelry: laughter, whoops and singing amidst music, before silence. Despite Caller's initial punitive intention to tutor his charges in 'regret', there is here a slight hint that relinquishing former patterns of definition may also offer some disburdenment: an acceptance of essential limitations.

The Glory Reel would seem to conclude Wells's texts for performance. Except that it doesn't.

2. Sailing to Walesland/Gwaliadir

Walesland/Gwaliadir was written by Wells during a two-year sailing trip, mostly alone, around the Mediterranean. This compounded epic, a poetic excavation of Wales's history from Neolithic times to the present, was published by Gomer Press in 2006, with a parallel translated text *yn Gymraeg* by Caryl Lewis. But even before it reached print, Charmian Savill directed a manifestation of the text for the stage, using many of the rehearsal devising techniques already mentioned in these commentaries. This was performed by students of Drama through the medium of Welsh in Aberystwyth University's Department of Theatre, Film and Television Studies Emily Davies Studio in May 2003, with the author present.

Walesland/Gwaliadir offers an obliquely surprising mythical-national epic, as Wells's *Wilderness* did for America(na), a brooding kaleidoscopic vision of 'histodust' and 'futurepast' (Wells and Lewis 2006: 3) which revolves and questions the dominant terms of so-called 'civilising effects', land, and love. I nominate *Walesland/Gwaliadir* as Wells's masterpiece, a profound and wry vision of political cultures clashing and forging: meanings communicated, dissolved, regenerated. Now that Wales has appointed both a National Theatre of Wales and a Theatr Gynedlaethol Cymru, companies which are intended to stage material of national import and distinctiveness (and may even occasionally collaborate), I hope that they might consider Wells and Lewis's texts as a basis for the fully professional staging they deserve: one day/*daw dydd*…

'Do we want solid words? Or do we want to smash the solidity of words?' asks the theatre director Eugenio Barba (Barba 1995: 138). His consideration of this question, and the possibility of a 'dialectic of apotheosis and derision' (*ibid*, 141), blasphemy and devotion, suggests properly ambitious objectives for theatre, and for poetry. It also identifies the dialectic in which many of Wells's fictional protagonists find themselves, and others. We see and hear these characters try to construct (self-)mesmeric carapaces; and how their intentness of focus suggests, provokes, perhaps even secretly desires, their own antitheses. This is language deployed as self-begetting estrangement, or even derangement; although, as Brendan Kennelly observed, 'when you're deprived of the factor that could drive you mad, you're truly alone then' (Kennelly, in Pine 1994: 185). Wells's characters are essentially in a restless, peculiar, *poetic* dialogue with themselves, usually more so than with others. It is natural that this leads them (and their performers and audiences) into dark and abject territories, that are alien to the demonstrative and reconciliatory patterns of earlier 'poetic drama' (as more conventionally associated with the early Twentieth Century theatre works of Auden and Isherwood, Eliot, Fry and MacNeice).

Kennelly sees, and proposes, a more vitally anarchic purpose in and for poetry:

> Poetry tends to recognize and demonstrate what a conventional morality will tend to outlaw and condemn. The imagination, when it is probing, serves no system, obeys no law but its own longing for exciting truth [...] To try to inhibit or limit that function is to do violence to the very nature of poetry, to make it the sweet, biddable, musical slave of our expectations. (Kennelly 1994: 44)

The curiously probing impulse of this poetry is the heartbeat of a truly searching drama: a drama which incorporates the hunger and generosity, as well as the fear and violence, of which the human soul is capable. Wells's texts for performance offer practitioners and audiences the mysterious challenge which Peter Brook discovers at the heart of theatre: 'Theatre is always both a search for meaning and a way of making this meaning meaningful for others' (Brook 1993: 76).

After all, Wells's writing suggests, words are not only limitations: though these may prove fatal, 'word*skill*' indeed (a compound noun I borrow from an engraving by Alan Halsey which adorns Wells's writing desk). Words are constructions to promise mutuality, permit joint endeavour, providing means to overturn the inhibition of dominant definitions: homeopathic poisons to reverse pressures, to turn things and people into their opposites, alchemical means to realize the rationally impossible: as crystallized by Wells's poem 'The Dumps':

> For see now, from
>
> This self-inflicted weal
>
> How cleverly I sicken
>
> How easily I heal

(Wells 1988: *Just Bounce* 3)

Words are one of the defining features of human thought and action, yet they defy generalization. They are cunningly made, potentially so skillful in their effects as to be overlooked, and therefore wily, secretive, illicit; yet decisive manifestations of what can be effected with both artful dexterity and hidden import: *sly deeds...*

THE GLORY REEL

A Comedy

Characters

PLAYER   A Holy Sister

DANCER   An Outlaw

CALLER   An Owl

Commissioned by Clive Meachen and Douglas Houston, for Aberystwyth University's season of 'Verbals' productions. Performed at Aberystwyth Arts Centre 1996, with the following participants:

PLAYER: Sister P

DANCER: Will Kaufman

CALLER: Nigel Wells

Music   Brouhaha orchestra

                       (Nick Jones, Nick Taylor, Peter Pavli)

Design   Meri Wells and Steve Mattison

Direction   Michael Bodenstein

THE GLORY REEL

MUSICIANS:

        Once would we stand
        gloved hand in bare hand
        sip our carafed wine
        and pleasantly through time
        stand perfectly in line
        and then we fall.

        And a certain crudeness taints the lips
        a hint of lewdness squints the eyes
        the skin of cream or skin of tan
        is revealed by a thing that quips
        and jokes at this creation
        that caused the great commotion
        but withholds any potion
        though promises us lotion bye and bye.

        Once would we run
        stripped down for the sun
        wrapped up for the moon
        paint our burn to a tune
        trace shape from a loon
        and then we fall.

        And a stripping soreness splits the lips
        a stinging rawness smarts the eyes
        the skin so pink or skin so wan
        upon the woman or the man
        is reclaimed by the thing that quips
        and jokes at all creation
        that causes all commotion
        and will not issue potion
        just promises us lotion bye and bye.

Once would we dance
styled for hope or for chance
tap the toe or the heel
catch her glance or his feel
so leisurely heal
and then we fall.

And a walking blackness puffs the lips
the skin of fair or skin of dun
upon the woman or the man
is reviled by that thing that quips
and damns its joke creation
that likes to cause commotion
that loves a bright cremation
that never hands out potion
but maybe dabs on lotion bye and bye
just maybe drips some lotion on the lips
just maybe sluices lotion in the eye
yes please prepare the lotion now we die
oh please prepare that lotion for we fly.

Scene: someplace.

DANCER is testing the edge of a knife. PLAYER is idly swinging a rosary. DANCER is bloodstained, a short scrap of rope around his neck. PLAYER's face is streaked with black, her habit is scorched, charred.

PLAYER   Hello there

DANCER   Uh

PLAYER   How's it goin'

DANCER   Uh

PLAYER   Good song

DANCER   Yuh

PLAYER   Been here a while then?

DANCER   Yuh

PLAYER   Me too

DANCER   Hmm

PLAYER   So what happens now?

DANCER   Uh

PLAYER   I mean, were you going to do anything, you know, do you fancy making a move there or anything?

DANCER   Uh

PLAYER   What do you think? It's been a while

165

DANCER	I guess
PLAYER	So, do you have a plan at all?
DANCER	Uh - I guess . . . I guess the plan'd be to hang around here till ya cain't stand it any longer - then go someplace else and hang around.
PLAYER	Well - a good plan mister
DANCER	Yeah - well to hell with it
PLAYER	*(makes dismissive gesture)* Whisht !
	(music)
CALLER	*(off)* Flack it - flack it, flock it and fluck it. *(enters furiously flapping at himself)* Bastard. Steaming bastard, piss-driven, flacking hell-fire. An owl, a sniffing owl. Jesus Jane Christ, what a clout - ah look at this shit – I said, not feathers, nothing with feathers. I hate flacking feathers. Nothing with feathers thanks very much your cloutship I said - none of the feathered variety thank you - scales as usual please oh cloutish one - yes? Dog wife. I've always had scales and she flanking well knows it. Scales are what I'm good in - scales are me - they all know that - she knows that. But no, our clever clit, great omnipotent, I'm in charge royal madam minge trap decides feathers. Shite - I could've stood skin - stuck fur, but, pricking louse-bound mythological bastard feathers . . . flack it. And - I don't believe her – a tossing owl of all things - transparent sow, I know what she's up to – good choice ma'am – it's always the clacking nightshift round here

166

anyway. Jesus - what she knows about labour relations would rattle in a gnat's arse.

However, however, I'm professional - precious little respect I get for it though –

if it's on the flicking job sheet I do the flicking job. *(waggles his wings)* Jeez, how do you work these flackers?

You what? *(answering unheard voice from off)* Alright, alright I'm going - *(mutters)* too wit too clucking woo to you too madaam *(louder)* right too wit too woo - I'm on my way. *(takes clipboard from pocket in wings - consults – while examining Dancer and Player who are oblivious to him.)* Ok - we're on the job - let's have a look here.

Subject: male - *(indicates DANCER's genitals with pencil)* one, two - check *(ticks job sheet).*
Condition: damaged – yes *(ticks job sheet).* Case notes: Outlaw - entry point south western United States - butcherer of men, women and children, both native and white, guilty and innocent, singly and in groups.

Killer for money, goods and sport, in anger or with humour, of any creature drawing breath - without distinction.

Desecrator and destroyer of buildings - private, commercial, religious. Defiler, both sexually and with proprietary implements, of beings human and animal, living and dead.

Known to have fashioned - from victim's body parts - internal and external - artefacts of personal adornment.

Also to have indulged partiality for flesh of human infants white, raw or cooked.

Well - you're a lad aren't you eh?
Let's see - manner of exit: shot and hanged, hmm no surprise there *(studies job sheet)* no details

167

though - pity, helps to have a bit of background -
still, no matter, we can work it accordingly.

Now then - recommendation: The Glory Reel - well I
suppose they'd have to - no option really.

Right now - over here *(flips pages of clipboard)*
What have we got?

Subject: female - *(indicates PLAYER's breasts and
genitals with pencil)* two, one - check *(ticks job
sheet)*. Condition: damaged yes *(ticks job sheet)*.
Case notes: Holy sister - Order of the blessed
Norah Ni Mhurchu - a missionary order - about the
Lord's work - entry point: settlement of San Juan
Perez United States/Mexico border via country of
Ireland, northwest coastal area - turned feral -
cause unspecified. Acquired prodigious and
depraved appetites - addiction to debauchery. Eater
of own and others' excrement - unremitting thirst
for liquor, urine, sanctified wine - cocktails of
same. Claimed in basest form sexual service
indiscriminately of male and female adults - native
or white - encouraged lewd and grotesque
behaviour amongst children in place of worship -
sought physical congress with animals and with
snakes - besmirched with female fluids holy relics
of the Blessed Nora Ni Mhurchu.
George Henry Jesus - got a pair here alright -
where do they find 'em? Now - manner of exit:
confined in a dry latrine, covered with brushwood
and burnt *(laughs)*. Could happen to anyone. And -
recommendation: sure to be - yes - The Glory
Reel. Well - feathers aside I will say it's a proper
job - you don't give this sort of thing to the
frocking apprentice, oh no.
(puts away clipboard - claps hands)
Right then my little tear-arses

we'd best get started then -
hands off cocks onto socks,
behave and don't piss me off, ok.

PLAYER   So *(to DANCER)* about your plan . . .

DANCER   Yuh

CALLER   Oi *(hits PLAYER on the side of head and in almost the same movement kicks DANCER's legs from under him)* I'm your
flacking plan you fluckers - I'm plan A, plan B and the flacking contingency plan as well, alright. Sorry, sorry - bit of overreaction there - I do lose the old feather duster sometimes - got off to a bad start today see - hassle from upstairs and these feathers are giving me gyp.

Whatever - now - things are running a little late - I should have been here for your arrival - would have been if it wasn't for the feather business. So - best try and catch up - bit of a recap - I'll make a note - there - alright? - off we go.

(PLAYER and DANCER stir, stretch and scratch)

PLAYER   Hello there

DANCER   Howdy

PLAYER   Did we meet already

DANCER   Cain't say - yuh well - seems like

PLAYER   That's a strange thing for you

DANCER   Seen stranger

PLAYER	Yes - well then it's an interesting life you've been leading there mister
DANCER	Ain't dull I reckon
PLAYER	Ach and sure me own now has on occasion been lively but - no bones now - there was - you know - something seems - no bones - a wee bit - do you not feel - think now - peculiar here?
DANCER	Well - a mite - I guess
PLAYER	I would say so mister I would - and how come - tell me this now - how come it does seem - listen now - I do not know at all - listen now - here from there - or from anywhere - or nowhere - at all, at all - tell me that if you like
DANCER	Don't recollect huh?
PLAYER	I do not
DANCER	Well hell - you were just never here before
PLAYER	That's true for you but, mister hon – ears on now - I don't recall the travelling - I don't recall buying a wee ticket - blanketing a mule - lacing boots and bags – I don't recall the journey or the getting here - so I don't
DANCER	Guess you just disremembered
PLAYER	Well sure and that's possible – things have been a whisk hazy the while - on and off you know
DANCER	The hell you say

PLAYER	But. I don't think, look - yourself now – I don't see you having too much in the way of transportation there
DANCER	Surely ain't
PLAYER	C'mon then mister hon - what's the story here eh? Look myself now - I was having a nice wee walk with some interesting theological scholars when - the Blessed Norah forgive them - they got themselves terrible over excited. For my own well- being and reputation you know, I felt obliged to leave the discussion, but then, on account of the insistence of their argumentative natures, was forced to flee their company and eventually to take refuge in a bit of a hole along by the bare road where I do believe I had a wee faint
DANCER	The hell you did
PLAYER	As I recall I would say so though do you know mister dear I'm starting wondering now if this, you know, peculiarity and maybe yourself there also are not just after being a wee thingum of a dream here - brought on by the small measures of watered wine I have recently been taking for the female complaint - the Blessed Norah forgive us that thing – it is recommended by the visiting Father for such occasions but truth to tell you can't always trust its quality or condition
DANCER	The hell you can't
PLAYER	Indeed - but your own self now - come on and look thoughtful honey dear
DANCER	I guess, I guess - well hell I reckon I took a knock on the head when my horse fell - like yourself there

I had to light out - bein' pursued by a bunch of rapscallions right enough – we was discussin' prices in a store - neighbourly as it seemed an' they took agin my recommendation - got right prickly and like I say I had to light out and then my horse - over she goes and, well there you have her - that's about the full bag of dust I reckon

PLAYER   Well an' all

DANCER   'less o' course you could be trackin' right there, lady - that store you know - sell cactus alcohol with a bug in her - stuff'll put you in a dream sure'n a greased forty four

PLAYER   Well an' all

CALLER   So - a little puzzled eh - a tsk confused - not quite sure what in hell's happening hmm - that's ok - you should fit in well 'round here - anyway all will, I'm told, be revealed in due course - I'm told

DANCER   'scuse me

CALLER   Yes, yes

DANCER   Do I know you fella?

CALLER   Know me, know me - ha ha very good

DANCER   Hell *(spits)*

CALLER   Ha ha - excellent, excellent

PLAYER   Well indeed that's a sorry enough spectacle you'd not want to be knowing at all mister dear

CALLER   One moment please *(makes note on clipboard)* continue

PLAYER	You think it's something got out from somewhere?
DANCER	Hell just a drunk idjit
CALLER	Not an idiot and not drunk - chance'd be a fine thing - no dear hearts and gentle people, honoured guests - I am your appointed guide, spiritual and medical adviser, friend and confident - I also arrange music, supply good condition used clothing and dispose of waste material - you will learn to love me and I will teach you regret - any question?
PLAYER	I was dreaming
DANCER	I was dreaming
CALLER	'fraid not folks - you weren't and you're not
PLAYER	I took refuge
DANCER	I fell
CALLER	No and no
PLAYER	Thin wine
CALLER	No
DANCER	Bug juice
CALLER	No
DANCER	I don't get it
PLAYER	What is . . .

CALLER	Like I said - a tsk confused eh – well it will only get worse *(laughs)*. Now if you wouldn't mind please - we don't need these do we *(he removes gun from DANCER's holster and rosary from PLAYER)* - part and parcel you know *(wrapping rosary around gun and putting in wing pocket)* - well that's what she'd say *(nodding to offstage)* what a radical thinker, huh.
DANCER	You took my gun
CALLER	Fancy
DANCER	How did you do that?
CALLER	*(in extravagantly formal voice)* By the authority invested in me . . .
DANCER	No - how did - why didn't I . . .
CALLER	'Cos *(mimics DANCER as John Wayne parody)* "your hide belongs to me pilgrim" that's why – feel like a short stroll hmm?
PLAYER	I said this was peculiar - look mister bird-thing now could you please tell me and your man there who or what you are and where and why we are - 'cos to be honest this is getting a wee bit tiresome
CALLER	Ooh my
DANCER	No one ever took my gun
CALLER	Tiresome eh ha - *(again mimicking)* "well that's kinda how things are around here little missy" - if you know what I mean - *(mimics PLAYER in stage Irish)* "but don't you be frettin' yourself there now alright". Look,

we've got a right old distance to cover so why
don't we get going and I can tell you - or with a
little encouragement - you can tell me - all about it
- on the way alright

DANCER   I'd kinda appreciate where we're going first bird

PLAYER   Indeed

CALLER   Going - going - where do you think we're going -
              we're going dancing

(They go off or lights go down)

MUSICIANS:

There is a list of consequences, things undone in
kingdom come.
The very list that could explain the pain,
the dark beneath the sun
And that list was left here somewhere
But we can't quite remember just where
Though we could write our own list to replace it
did we dare.

There is a handle made to open anything
that has been closed
Another handle made to strangle any queries that are posed
And is that handle with our hand on
The one that slacks off or only winds on
Or is that hand not really our hand? – moving on…

There is a queue that we should queue in as
we've little else to do
But queue in front of another queue that only queues
to join a queue
So can we please form a further queue near
The other queue that has formed where

This queue joins the rear of the queue
that's queueing here.

There is a plug that is freed to feed the water
to the drain
Another plug that is fixed to seal the laughter
in the brain
But when that drain is blocked and stinking
And smiles and laughter are all shrinking
The Devil's plumber is at work –
and God is winking.

*(PLAYER and DANCER reappear - heads bowed –
CALLER leading them in litany)*

CALLER	We who are selected
DANCER	endure and offer
PLAYER	lacklustre confession
CALLER	We who are selected
DANCER	bear with patience
PLAYER	all earthly emblems
CALLER	We who are selected
DANCER	we are penitent and inconsolable
PLAYER	we are desolate and incomplete
CALLER	We who are selected
DANCER	in our frayed and hollow coats
PLAYER	emerge from those remnants of error

CALLER	We who are selected beg license
D & P	disencumbered of inscription, artistry and all devices of candour and heroism
CALLER	beg and do agitate for
DANCER	private and visible
PLAYER	diffused and finite
CALLER	the decay of endeavour
D & P	acrid and interminable
CALLER	the abandonment of expectation
D & P	its dry and muffled corrosion
CALLER	the entanglement of appointment
D & P	that calligraphy of insult
CALLER	We who are selected
PLAYER	distanced from fluency
DANCER	pigment and mannerism obsolete
PLAYER	crave knowledge now
DANCER	claim influence on
CALLER	all in all
D & P	the eiderdown and the birthmark, the connoisseur and the decent fellow, the shy salute and the sinewy bride,

the polished deliberation
and the corridor wherein it dulls

CALLER   We reject - speedily and with venom

PLAYER   the ulcer and the yawn

DANCER   which spellbind

PLAYER   combine

DANCER   as failed and wretched dream

CALLER   We who are selected conclude

D & P   tremble and conclude

CALLER   all in all

D & P   conclude

(CALLER makes note on clipboard)

CALLER   Hold up folks - let's take the weight off
for a moment shall we - park yourselves down here
(they sit) – have a sandwich
(he produces some - they eat).

You know personally I would like to discontinue
some of the formal stuff- but whats-her-grots is
dead keen on tradition so who am I to argue -
though I might say that at the last AGM I made my
views known in no uncertain terms

PLAYER   Your views - I have views - what of my views bird my . . .

DANCER   My views are *(he stands)* you tricked me down -
got me powerless – took my gun - and for that I

will - and you better believe it - gut you like the chicken you are. For a dumb cluck with a beak you have a big mouth

CALLER

Fine, fine - well let me put it this way *(he stands)* one: *(he jabs DANCER's chest with each word)* you shouldn't interrupt when someone else is speaking - two: *(he grasps DANCER's crotch)* as you say – you are powerless *(he pushes him back to sitting position)* - three: *(CALLER raises both his arms)* I'm the cranking comedian 'round here thanks very much *(turns to PLAYER while resuming seat)*. You were saying my dear?

PLAYER

My view was and is that this whole business is either a particularly confused dream or a mild hallucination brought on by whatever causes and mister bird I can tell you that being a strong-minded woman I have every intention of rolling over and thinking of something else whereupon, as I am not in the habit of recalling bouts of indigestion you mister quack doodle will very quickly become less than a memory of a memory

CALLER

(throws sandwich at her) Oh cluck off – d'you know you're becoming very longwinded – d'you know that. Anyway according to this *(indicates clipboard)* you rolled over and thought of something else one thousand four hundred and sixty times during the space of one calendar year - not an obvious career move for someone of your vocation I would say. One thousand four hundred and sixty . . . let's see, that's four times a day you rolled over you rascal you and *(checks clipboard)* I'm none too sure as to how often you were actually thinking of something else you know.

Christ, I've had Popes and Cardinals here
who've only rolled over four times in a year –
mostly of course they were thinking of something else -
physical necessity if you catch my drift –
however, never mind that - look, we must press on –
if you've finished

(puts remnants of sandwiches in pocket) –
we'll go a little further and then sweetness
and light here *(indicates PLAYER)* WILL recall her
indigestion for us.
(They stand and take up litany position)

CALLER	Upon our journey
DANCER	we are compound, malicious, frightful
CALLER	Upon our journey
PLAYER	we are quick, breathless, electrical
CALLER	Stepping our comfortless way
D & P	we are severed, random, bereft
CALLER	Diamond complexity
DANCER	smother our substance
CALLER	Charitable instrument of obscurity
PLAYER	unmake our text
CALLER	Curtain of immensity
DANCER	we are embittered of finesse
PLAYER	we are diverted from sonority

180

CALLER   and plead correction

D & P   upon our journey

              (They walk a little - then stop –
              CALLER looks at clipboard)

CALLER   So there you were *(they move apart –*
              DANCER and PLAYER with heads bowed) giving
              yourself a bit of a Jeffrey *(makes motion of female*
              masturbation) then what happened?

PLAYER   *(raises head and, entranced, speaks)*
              She is a poor girl from a poor parish where sea and
              rock, dark jaw-locked, ravage then relent.
              Of choice she is much alone - she spoons her name
              in earth - she smiles as rain erases her - smears and
              muddies her - proper behaviour from the weather –
              "good weather" she cries "good weather".

              Once, a young one cutting turf called out to her –
              touched her here. She liked that - but found her own
              hand more adept. Curious, she dipped and tasted of
              herself – thereafter frequently drew sustenance –
              from that deep well, from that   dark store.
              She is a poor girl from a poor parish.

              She goes with the sisters - lives that hard regime:
              Ravage then relent. She is much alone –
              the bones of her nose become tender –
              her tongue hurts. Sight, hearing, touch retreat,
              detach - she thinks one day she'll not
              remember them - taste and smell overwhelm her.
              She hunts out refuse, haunts the laundry bins –
              she scoops from the spoil-heap's crusted slops
              her bidden name - delights and shudders

at that seepage of herself. She maintains her secrecy . .
.she . . . is . .is
(her speech slows - her head lowers)

CALLER   Shit *(takes notes)* - Oi! whacker
(kicks DANCER lightly) -
help out for a moment, there's a good lad

DANCER   *(head raises)* . . . embarked for a convertible territory -
under trust from her order - she has maintained her
secrecy - she floats free - the sea and heaven wrack
her, she hoards her stomach's voidance - returns to
it and is restored. In the hull's profundity - from
rope tat, caulking pot – she gleans cosmetic stuff -
tars her nails a rich and reckless black.
A sailor - in her weakness - and his dark – forces her –
takes her from behind
(CALLER mimes lewdly) –
later she probes her fingers there - her nostrils yawn
for odour then – saliva drips for taste

CALLER   *(slaps DANCER on the back of the head –
DANCER lowers head)* Ok, ta - that'll do *(lifts
PLAYER's head - slaps each cheek)* Alright now?

PLAYER   She entertains - in the deep bilge -slakes a bold
thirst – with salt crew - certain deck passengers -
between times marvelling - marvelling

CALLER   *(writes)* mar - vell - ing

PLAYER   Tainted diet, sour prayer - hold her in thrall - she is
much alone

CALLER   Uh huh *(makes note)*

PLAYER   Sensationalised - she is a miracle and much alone

CALLER   Yes

PLAYER   Disembarked - Westernport for San Juan Perez - the
                desert traverse - aridity - desert smells are subtle - the
                tastes few - she breathes her mount –
                and her lone guide at night - soon –
                she tastes him - tangible language
                rears from the pores - spreads - dries - the desert
                also craves -

CALLER   Ok - look - let me just get this - straight so far -
                yeah - you're brought up short on food and home
                comforts. Right - you're a solitary, right - you
                develop a need and a taste or something different -
                you follow your nose, right - subsequently you take
                the sniff and lick option, sidelining in unusual and
                prohibited sexual activity while pursuing a
                vocational career with a religious order, right - so
                then *(writing)* - poverty, pornography, fetishism,
                blasphemy and - let's see - confession - excuse -
                contrition - or what or what - hm?

DANCER   Or what - or what shall it profit a man
                that he inherit the earth and forfeit his soul

CALLER   *(hits DANCER)* Oh flacking hell –
                shut up can't you, I'm trying to concentrate here -
                anyway that's completely out of character *(jabs at
                clipboard - turns to PLAYER)* - now

PLAYER   . . . what - what the desert - what the poor girl from
                the poor parish her order and its mission - what
                they crave

CALLER   Well . . . so . . .

PLAYER   Her feet are diminutive –
                the desert is said to be vast -
                it may be - or may not –

it fails to claim her attention -
she lives a small circumference –
she is diameter – she hoopla's, cartwheels,
whirligigs - home place –
far place rest place . . .

CALLER   *(puts hand over PLAYER's mouth)*
                  Hold it - hold it - your
                  mouth's starting to get ahead of your brain dear –
                  anyway that about brings it up to date –
                  the rest seems fairly well documented here
                  (indicating clipboard) - any blanks can be filled in as
                  and when.

                  So then babes
                  *(puts arms around PLAYER and DANCER's
                  shoulders - gives a squeeze)*
                  what d'ya say - off we jolly well once more and
                  you need to be limbering up anyway - you've no
                  chance if you're all stiff and clumpy - so why don't
                  we nudge on with a touch of the old quick step
                  then, when we next stop for a breather, knobrot
                  here can tell us the story of his life which I don't
                  doubt will be a wonderment - right then - best foots
                  forward *(makes note)* dim dum dim dum dam *(lines
                  up PLAYER and DANCER)* matthew mark - hot
                  foot left foot - go
                  *(They start to jog - call and response as in a
                  soldier's marching rhymes)*

CALLER   Jigalong jogalong move it along

P & D   Jogalong jigalong singing a song

CALLER   Sweeter the song the better you go

P & D   Angel turned us quick and slow

CALLER	Best be nimble best be quick
P & D	Angel carries an angel stick
CALLER	Best trip lightly 'cos you know
P & D	Angel is a so and so
CALLER	Swing your jugs or swing your dong
P & D	Jogalong jigalong won't be long
CALLER	Till you tread the stepping floor
P & D	Angel stamps and claps his claw
CALLER	And with a hup two three four life love death law hup six seven eight work plan crime fate assembly halt Here we are - nearly there - stand easy – squat on your bots if you like here *(passes around a bottle of pop)* – sip-a slurp- for-all-this. So young killer-me-lad - tell us all about it.
DANCER	Huh
CALLER	You know - your life an' all
DANCER	Shit - a kid you know - growin' an' such - doin' stuff - yuh know - kid stuff - hell – what's to say
CALLER	Well, try

DANCER   Dunno – cain't recollect - something - whip work -
                    hard company - best of the bad - the . . . hell I
                    dunno - what's to say - haul off will yuh

CALLER   Suit yourself, suit yourself –
                    that'll have to do then - p'rhaps
                    be ok - who knows - no fluff of my arse –
                    let's see - *(writes on clipboard)* 're - cal - ci – trant'.
                    Now then - I'm going to have to leave you
                    to talk amongst yourselves for a while –
                    I need to nip round the bend a ways –
                    have a dump - cough up a few pellets - ho ho - well not
                    really – I have to check if everything is laid on
                    properly – alright - see you later yeah –
                    have fun with the misery – back in a bit *(exits)*

                    (pause)

DANCER   I don't get it - I wouldn't have thought twice –
                    one shot -
                    (pulls knife from boot - tests edge) a few nicks
                    and he'd be
                    a money pouch - I don't get it

PLAYER   Peculiarity - a peculiarity –
                    *(she sniffs the air - rubs fingers
                    in armpit, sniffs and licks them)*
                    I smell pale - taste flat -
                    a peculiarity - improper

DANCER   I never did those especially - smell, taste yuh know -
                    in the gun trade what you work on most are - sight and
                    hearing - the pulled pistol - the sneak-up - snick of
                    metal flick of skin - yeah, mostly the eye and the
                    ear - mostly.

186

PLAYER	And that's about the mostly you've said above the necessary do you know that - you're not a man for conversation or the chat - are you mister?
DANCER	Mostly - I keep close
PLAYER	Mostly - so sometimes . . .?
DANCER	Sometimes what?
PLAYER	So - sometimes - you trot the talk
DANCER	Talk?
PLAYER	Mm talk - words - flying - away and back – this face to that
DANCER	Ain't too set on that *(pause)* - sometimes – sometimes I say muh piece
PLAYER	Piece?
DANCER	Muh poem
PLAYER	Poem?
DANCER	Yuh - poem - gotta poem - muh piece
PLAYER	The Blessed Norah - aren't you the surprise
DANCER	Huh
PLAYER	And were you making this - piece – learning it or who
DANCER	Couldn't say
PLAYER	But how are you knowing it?

DANCER	Just do - always have - always have
PLAYER	The Blessed Norah - so who do you say this poem to - when?
DANCER	When's right - whoever - I guess *(pause)*
PLAYER	'Course a poem's not conversation
DANCER	Look shit - dunno - hell - quit will yuh *(pause)*
PLAYER	I'd say - this piece - time could be right – you know - now
DANCER	Hell
PLAYER	Not sure - couldn't say - but . . .
DANCER	Look - 'nuff said
PLAYER	Come on with you
DANCER	Now don't you press - I'm a dark man
PLAYER	And I'm a fierce girl and you go pale and I doubt your old piece
DANCER	Look
PLAYER	Whisht!
DANCER	Hell *(goes for his gun - but his holster is empty)* hell - look *(jabs finger in PLAYER's direction)* look . . . hell
PLAYER	Ha

(pause)

188

DANCER	Ok
PLAYER	What?
DANCER	Ok - listen
PLAYER	Ok
DANCER	Ok
PLAYER	Ears on - away
DANCER	Ok

(pause)

'S muh piece - er – hm:

Cowboys come and hear a story of the power
and the glory. Of death and great adventure,
shining crime How it was for one gunslinger side
by side with his dead ringer. Beyond the law,
below that border line

Oh any one of four or five, near two parts dead
just half alive
Would recognise the tale I have to tell
Most any of the top-notch guns, the badland's
universal sons
Would know I say it true and say it well

It was in the town of Gutshot,
Sheriff Johnson tied the hang-knot
And placed it round the neck of someone's pa
Then he slapped old Dollar's butt end
and so lawfully he did send
That pappy where a light shone deep and far

And legal-like the neck snapped, and festive
like the crowd clapped
An artist chalked a likeness of the head
The soul strung for the bye and bye,
heard as it flew a tiny cry
Somewhere was birthed a boy child in its stead

That boy then came to his damned senses grew and
grew and learned his tenses
Learned how to walk the line but walk it skew
Learned the word and learned to figure, learned the
blade and learned the trigger
Learned what his other self already knew

The boy became the youth, the man - a man hid
from a youth who ran
From a boy's dark fright at a deep far light
A man shored up by shadow stuff, in double time,
at double bluff
Just fighting life and living for a fight

For that deep far light honed his sight, as his
hearing tuned to the night
While anger rolled and rattled round his brain
By skin and the body bones caged, his nerve ends
and arteries raged
Is pain the only thing to ease the pain

A voice sighed like a smoking gun, now listen good
there is no fun
This is as good as it will get by far
That voice cut like a Barlow knife,
there is no other better life
Believe me, I'm your brother and your pa

The man became the thing he was because of this
and just because
And that's the way it happens, well I guess

It's kind of like that I should say, a bit like that
or that- away
Yeah, that's the way it happens, more or less

When you're born out of a dying,
ghosts come round with truth and lying
And put you right and likewise put you wrong
That's the blood and that's the theory,
thanks to all of you who hear me
That's the end of this interesting song.

S muh piece

PLAYER   Well - ya boy yuh - that was grand –
                fair play to youse - 'cept it sort of tailed off - you
                didn't miss a bit did you?

DANCER   (shouts) 'Smuh piece

PLAYER   Alright, alright don't be going mad

DANCER   Yeah, well, don't you be winding me

PLAYER   Phuff!

                (They stand in silence for a moment)

                Aye well (she again rubs armpits - sniffs and licks
                fingers) Hmm (she looks at DANCER - stamps her
                feet and quickly draws two imaginary pistols which
                she shoots with gunshot noises at DANCER - he is
                unresponsive - she holsters pistols – moves closer
                to DANCER and claps hands - DANCER slowly
                raises head to look at her)

DANCER   Huh

PLAYER	Aye, well - I conclude we've lost some senses mister hon - I do conclude
DANCER	No, no couldn't be - don't wind me - don't say - don't be maddening me *(jabs at her chest)*
PLAYER	And don't you be getting brackish on me - don't be going nasty
DANCER	Nasty is as nasty jumps
PLAYER	Well your man the bird was saying - was he saying - I believe he was saying - you were the jumping boy
DANCER	Yeah, clean, straight and nasty - miss weird - damn birdbrain marked you for some queer weirdness - the queerest - did he not - surely did
PLAYER	Surely no - I would argue a serene gratification found in the living body - a God shaped artefact - and argue - sister self- blessed with certain heightened senses - worships at the fount and font of that - a Christian undertaking - I do not shoot out eyes, slit gizzards, eat babies or hang tongues and fingers round my neck - so don't be talking now - there's a queer dear
DANCER	*(again jabbing)* Don't you be - don't you be – don't you be maddening me
PLAYER	Whisht! away and suck your bum mister queer dear
DANCER	Agh *(draws knife and stabs at PLAYER's stomach – as knife point nears stomach it is brought up short as though by an invisible wall - he tries again - and again - looks at knife with horror then hurls it away - examines hand – groans and sobs)* - ah I don't get it *(he slowly sinks to his knees)*

PLAYER *(holds his head against her)* There mister - don't be now Don't be *(she kneels in front of him strokes and pets him)* Don't be taking on now - it's peculiarity - just so – there *(becomes aroused - sniffs him - licks the fingers she strokes him with - shows frustration as she cannot smell or taste)* Ah honey dear - we are not working - we are not what we were - we are insipid and glum
(They hug and roll around - in comfort rather than passion though they would wish the latter)

Ah, what's to be done honey dear?
speak in one language - speak it clear

DANCER *(makes savage and inarticulate sounds)*

SINGERS/MUSICIANS:

He never had comfort from talk
he spoke as the snake or the hawk
the strike out of silence
conversational violence
discussing your child with his fork

He never had much truck with words
they flew from him as might small birds
or itched in his arse
like wipings of grass
and dropped to the earth with his turds

The plum in the mouth and the peach
were not his preferred mode of speech
his lips moved infernal
the rhymes all internal
and right to the heart they would reach

Body language of dark innocence

193

delivered with fine eloquence
would speak to the blood
unlock its rich flood
only never though in the past tense

So - a song just to commemorate
the outlaw's dark alphabet
where the language of rage
never reaches the page
and murder is articulate

PLAYER   Oh mister dear fear
we were warm we were bold
we are lame we are cold

SINGERS/MUSICIANS:

Oh there was little country girl
she went from there to here
well her eyesight wasn't up to much
and she'd only half an ear
but she'd a nose upon her
that would make the devil dream
and a mouth that held a tongue you'd bet
would make the devil cream

Diddly idle deedle idle deedle diddly idle dee
diddly idle deedle idle deedle diddly idle dee
diddly idle deele idle deedle diddly idle dee
diddly idle deedle idle deedle diddly idle dee

Oh she got into a habit
was as good as it was bad
and she thumpered like a rabbit
any lass or thing or lad
but who can make a judgment stack
against such pretty acts
when the devil makes a pact with God

194

and neither has the facts

Diddly idle deedle idle deedle diddly idle dee
diddly idle deedle idle deedle diddly idle dee
diddly idle deedle idle deedle diddly idle dee
diddly idle deele idle deedle didly idle dee

DANCER	*(moans)*
PLAYER	We are not what we were
DANCER	I'm a dark man d'ys hear
PLAYER	So you were honey dear - so you were
DANCER	For the heart-coin - blood-pockets stitched into my coat
PLAYER	Aye, I don't doubt
DANCER	I ransack all - carry away - entrails and the green money
PLAYER	Sure you did - so you did
DANCER	The sound that makes - the sight that is
PLAYER	No more wee man
DANCER	I am a dark man - famously dark
PLAYER	I fear what you may be - what I

SINGERS/MUSICIANS:

Blessed lord oh we got bored so
we got strange and went to town
Blessed saviour, our behaviour

195

made us famous, well renowned
Sought out the psalms was taught by the psalms
got caught on the palms of the lord
Wrapped in the arms, was wrapt in the arms
got trapped in the arms of the lord

Angel came by, angel oh my
we tramp with him overground
Angel feathers lead us ever
till we hear that undersound

Sought out the psalms was taught by the psalms
got caught on the palms of the lord
Wrapped in the arms, was wrapt in the arms
got trapped in the arms of the lord
Clapped in the arms, got mapped in the arms
was slapped by the arms of the lord

*(PLAYER and DANCER sink to the ground
clutching each other - CALLER tumbles in - in
disarray)*

CALLER   Bastards *(to offstage)* - I didn't ask for it you know *(picks
                himself up - checks clipboard - looks at PLAYER
                and DANCER)* Oh clock me - I might have known
                - leave you for five minutes and you go and get
                clacking religion *(shakes head)* - I shouldn't bother
                - believe me . . . Now - they've been having word
                (nods to offstage) and it looks like I could really
                get shat on if you're not sorted soon so *(gestures
                for them to rise)* let's get a grip eh - any questions,
                now's the time - question time now. alright - c'mon
                let's go - else big boss twitch person'll be getting a
                power surge in her pants and there'll be hell to pay.

                (pause) Look. it's ok - I might be a bit rough and
                ready but I am capable of the grunting civilities
                you know - so come on ask away

(makes notes on clipboard throughout the following exchanges: pause)

DANCER   Am I a dark man?

CALLER   Dark you may not recognise

PLAYER   Am I a damned girl?

CALLER   Fine fine damnation

DANCER   You took my gun

PLAYER   My rosary

CALLER   Devices of aggression and or protection - apart from yours truly have little worth or meaning - around here

DANCER   Where the hell is here?

CALLER   Any of those - but not there

PLAYER   There being where?

CALLER   The place you are not now nor will ever be

DANCER   Talk sense

CALLER   Sense oh my - oh you'd know
                all about sense and senses,
                wouldn't you

PLAYER   He was a hard man *(touching DANCER)*

CALLER   Indeed

PLAYER   No more?

CALLER	Nail on the head dear
DANCER	I don't get it
PLAYER	I fear I do
CALLER	Indeed?
DANCER	Small arms and a big country a pal once said – that's a life and living - sound weaponry – a red and rising landscape -a decent hat – then brother it's roughshod and gutshot – hell on hooves and the devil's right hand – savage and true - men without women – keeping the land low - rock level – the scorpion brothers - swiping at the civilised heart - my pal said. He got to be a thinker though - I cut his backbone out - for dice - left his hide at dry-tit creek - I believe I did - cain't quite recall
CALLER	Memory and armament are forfeit
PLAYER	We're. . . dead aren't we?
CALLER	Frocking brilliant - that's the quickest anyone's twigged for ages - that's great - right, cutting the coy ambiguities and in answer to your question - answer number one: yes answer number two: yes - answer number three: frocking hell yes - you know, you've quite made my day
DANCER	Dead? - I made my getaway - took a knock – drunk maybe
PLAYER	*(shows DANCER his neck rope and bloody clothing)* Wee man - honey dear - you did not - lank string in a coward's knot - bloody bruise and tatty rag -

	(indicates his crotch) the inevitable stain - all disprove the life - mister-has-been - mister dear
DANCER	*(long pause - spits)* Well hell - I can live with that, been better than halfway there this whole life - truth is I feel a sight handier for having the truth of it - hell, blaze away y'all - let's git to the fire
PLAYER	Well good man yourself - that's a fine spirit on you - hear that bird?
CALLER	Oh yes
PLAYER	So
CALLER	Well - next thing
DANCER	Whoa there crapdoodle - you're a shitkicking son of a hoot owl's ass - yeah
CALLER	Well you're feeling livelier - but don't push it
DANCER	So what's the story here? *(indicates CALLER's feathers)*
PLAYER	A question for you
CALLER	Don't ask - comes with the job
DANCER	Job?
CALLER	Just a clocking job - don't ask
PLAYER	It was yourself said ask away
CALLER	*(pause)* Alright, alright – I work for the Induction Services Department of the Global Correction Division of the

Universal Resettlement Programme, an Independent
Agency – alright?

DANCER   The hell you do

CALLER   Yes - under contract

PLAYER   And? . . . *(indicates feathers)*

CALLER   Her idea *(indicates offstage)* –
I've always worn a snakeskin outfit –
boots, jacket, hat - scales you see - androgynous -- right
renewable - right for the job and looked flaking great.
Then shag-rag almighty - ms bleeding political nipples –
decides - reassessment of image - changing attitudes –
positive discrimination – load of bolarkus - and I get
stuck into clucking owl suit so as to promote 'aspects of
female wisdom' – the shit end of shite as usual –
it doesn't occur to her that the moon eyed gets are flea
ridden flecking outcasts that every other bastard
pecks the piss out of - dull nunt – all bright ideas and
forget about my employment conditions – flock her - and
flock flacking feathers

PLAYER   Ya boy yuh it's a fat tongue you have alright

DANCER   I don't get it

CALLER   Well you asked

PLAYER   So - now?

DANCER   Yeah

CALLER   So yes - a bit of preparation and you're away - first
though bit more admin *(taps clipboard)* I need -
your initial reaction - overall impression - and a
general response - ok.

Right, no looking or touching - other than that feel free.
(pause - PLAYER and DANCER look blank) Come on - don't cluck about - speak *(slight pause - CALLER jabs PLAYER and DANCER with a pencil in time to words)* speak - your - mind - please

PLAYER   Bemused

DANCER   Befuddled

PLAYER   Aroused

DANCER   Stricken

PLAYER   Amazed

DANCER   Stupefied

PLAYER   Un-nerved

DANCER   Un-manned

PLAYER   Ecstatic

DANCER   Stricken

PLAYER   A twist in the skin

DANCER   A curve in the mind

PLAYER   Never could not sin

DANCER   Never could be kind

PLAYER   This is turnabout

DANCER	This is standaround
PLAYER	This is absence
DANCER	This is severance
PLAYER	This, as beads or pence
DANCER	is no sense and is sense
PLAYER	Perhaps and possibly
DANCER	this is what we see *(They turn and hold each other)*
CALLER	I said - not to look or touch
DANCER	Drying on a pole
PLAYER	your clenching stones
DANCER	Crisping under coal
PLAYER	my buttered bones
CALLER	Well ok - as that was so concise I'll overlook the contact - very good - thank you, thank you. Now then nearly dance time - you can read I believe - correct?
PLAYER	Being a sister - yes
DANCER	*(slowly - remembering)* Long since - before - I was a mission boy - yeah I can read
CALLER	Good - take these *(hands out sheets of paper)* – recite and memorise
DANCER	Gent's right arm

PLAYER	Over lady's shoulder
DANCER	Holding left hands
PLAYER	Advance and retire
DANCER	House around
PLAYER	Swing in place
DANCER	Gent circle left
PLAYER	Lady to the right
DANCER	Swing in waltz hold
PLAYER	Go around twice
DANCER	Make an arch
PLAYER	Pass through
DANCER	Face partner
PLAYER	Sidestep left
DANCER	Square across
PLAYER	Slide in
DANCER	Crown the lady
PLAYER	Chain right
DANCER	Advance sideways
PLAYER	And bow

DANCER	Dance the body
PLAYER	Around to home
CALLER	Good - a few steps further *(relieves them of dance notes)* - now, best try and make you a bit presentable - usually a lost cause with you sticky enders - but I do what I can *(produces a clothes brush - tidies them as they speak)*
DANCER	Things kinda come and go around here Birdy
CALLER	Yeah, you've noticed eh - croaking horrible isn't it - what can you do though
DANCER	Tricky for you too huh
CALLER	Well . . .
PLAYER	So can you tell us any thing - you know – about - you know . . .
CALLER	'Fraid not - would if I could but I can't - all the job sheet says is - meet you at arrival - check and update current information - give specific instruction - and get you to the right door in a fit state - then wait
DANCER	Wait for what
CALLER	Plucked if I know - I'm normally off once you're in - they're probably just pissing me about - unless perhaps you're a special case
PLAYER	Were we that fierce
CALLER	Well - pretty much - but - not for me to judge

DANCER	In - in where?
CALLER	In there *(points to door - which now lights up)* – And I think it's time to go time - here you are *(he produces two bright red triangular scarves – ties as kerchief for DANCER and headscarf for PLAYER)* right that's the best I can do - so - kick off flick off - bye bye
	(ushers them towards the door)
PLAYER	Ach well mister - will we go
DANCER	Why not - happy trails
	(They enter - music - solo fiddle plays slow air - CALLER makes notes on clipboard then sits, stands strides restlessly - PLAYER and DANCER reappear arms linked from dance - they huddle in silent conversation – CALLER is agitated)
CALLER	So - how'd you get on - didn't sound like a reel to me - how'd it go?
	(PLAYER and DANCER turn and stare at him)
PLAYER	How did what go?
CALLER	You know - the . . . *(he makes dance movements)*
DANCER	The what?
	(PLAYER turn back to each other)
CALLER	Well that's tricking great that is – that's madam that is - that's tricking typical

PLAYER   *(to DANCER)* We'll be headin' then

DANCER   Hell yes - let's ride

                *(They start to exit - PLAYER touches
                DANCER's arm to halt and silently reminds him of
                something – he produces an envelope - gives it to
                PLAYER who takes it to CALLER)*

PLAYER   They said to give you this

                *(She returns to DANCER - they exit –
                CALLER looks at envelope is thoughtful - looks after
                PLAYER and DANCER)*

MUSICIANS:

                And a lifelessness will lick the lips
                a deadness leak into the eyes
                the skin of fair or skin of foul
                upon the angel or the owl
                is renamed by whatever dips
                a feather in black diction
                then scrawls that bad prescription
                which scrambles death and fiction
                which says your watch and station
                are not for the duration
                though when you get it filled it is a lie

                (CALLER reluctantly opens envelope - reads)

CALLER   Ah hell - ah - vindictive stunt ah - *(pause)* well frock
                it and you - shallow ally slitforbrain – see if I care

                (quieter and with less confidence)

                see if I care

(louder with bravado)

fluck art let's dance – yeah - well - just quacking watch me

(screws up letter - throws away - quieter again)

just watch

(takes deep breath and straightens himself - with bravado again – marches to door and knocks smartly upon it - door opens – he enters - door closes - music [The Glory Reel on several instruments] - noise - laughter - owl hoots door opens and owl suit is thrown out - door closes - music/noise stops abruptly – lights out.

END

SLY DEEDS: an Afterword

Clive Meachen

In 1990, in conjunction with the Aberystwyth Arts Centre and the English Department of Aberystwyth University, I asked Bill Sherman and Nigel Wells to give a poetry reading. Little did I realize that this would provide the seed-pulse not only for the 'Verbals' series of poetry readings but also of a remarkable set of performances pieces intimately connected to those readings. At this first event, Nigel asked me to act as a second voice in reading a contrapunctally-composed poem from his sequence, *Wilderness*. The result was both strange and compelling. In the layout of its printed form, *Wilderness* had already pushed the envelope of its silent page to extreme, forcing its readers into a cinematic recreation of the words on the page. Now we had another element, implicit in the form of the poems but hard to perform within the restrictions of the individual voice.

The poem sequence *Wilderness* subsequently provided the basis for Wells's first text for performance, when its dramatic possibilities were more fully explored through the collaborative energies of actors, designers, musicians and director. More than an afterthought, yet not entirely free from the restrictions of a primarily poetic text, the performance of *Wilderness* opened a new door to further possibilities.

David Ian Rabey has chronicled the history of the performances. My job here is to explore the verbal energies of the resulting texts. Any audience will notice not only the difficulty but also the darkness of these pieces: a kind of angular, medieval cavorting, almost as if they were flashbacks of an apocalypse which has already taken place: post-historical, twisted, fevered, unexplained. Lodged like some unwelcome but oddly familiar guests in the recesses at the back of the brain, these texts replay themselves after the event unfolding with nightmare inevitability. And, as in nightmares, such inevitability stems from a logic we sense but cannot account for, which suggests that darkness is a primary cause of the difficulty we face.

In these pieces, Nigel Wells has hitched his energies to a collaborative mixture of creative resources, many of which remain more openly in contact with the audience. Not that he has surrendered to the complacent consumerism of mass culture; his plays demand active engagement, a stretching of the faculties, and this alone ensures that they will hardly be popular, no matter how common the ingredients from which they are made. Yet there remains a real and feigned

209

generosity here, an attempt to create inclusive art, no matter how weird some of its impulse might otherwise seem to be.

Resurrection Men is the most accessible of the texts printed here, its ballad form and simple narrative structure offering a stripped down, carnivalesque version of a story which has attracted many others. In the age of trainers, vitamin supplements and breast transplants it may come as something of a surprise to be asked to encounter the story of Burke and Hare, products of a time of a time when life was cheap and science operated with aristocratic disdain for anything that lay outside its mechanistic tunnel vision.

As Doctor Knox charts the complexities of the heart and face but remains oblivious to the metaphorical extensions of his words into human space, don't we hear the perennial voice of scientific disinterest? When we encounter the helpless innocence of Jamie, do we hear the perennial victim? As for Burke and Hare, mired in their irritable but self-satisfied materialism: aren't they the true face of much that passes for business, eager to turn a profit, and resolutely ignorant of the consequences? Not that this play is an allegory; rather, in focussing so single-mindedly on its material it gathers a power which resonates beyond itself, proof of the mythological imagination which informs these writings.

Resurrection Men involved Wells in a deliberate casting away of many of the subtle splendours to be found in his earlier writing, thereby making room for the creative input offered by others. *That Slidey Dark* has a richer verbal texture, product of a growing confidence in the collaborative venture, more aware of the space a writer can claim as his own. This isn't to dismiss *Resurrection Men*, which retains the force of dramatised folk music, elemental and tough, its words opening to that middle ground between song and speech which characterizes the real glory of the medium. Cut off from the world of casual explanations, *Resurrection Men* isolates a historical moment and cuts it adrift from its context, but so that it floats free, as an image which reflects the glints of other historical periods: glints accumulating into a composite, historical picture of what it might be to be human. Ballad, mummer's play, nineteenth century broadsheet, twentieth century exposé, Hammer horror musical - all these fold into the singular act of accretion which constitutes the play. But *That Slidey Dark* offers an even richer composite. It steps more fully and deeply into its material and theatrical form, and the gains it makes are, I think, substantial. The dementia presented here echoes that of the earlier piece, even if its archaeology of that condition digs deeper, approaching the status of metaphysical horror, disquieting and absolute.

In a sense, *That Slidey Dark* is a version of the alchemical quest to reconcile the worlds of spirit and matter, but here the reconciliation is steeped in blackness rather than a redeeming shaft of light. All that escapes is a vagrant and useless cry of innocence, twin of Jamie's cry in *Resurrection Men*. The strangely beguiling happenstance of rhyme haunts *That Slidey Dark*, breaking open the gates of sense and syntax, dissolving words into animal sound, urgent and wounded. The man who approaches Dante's wood is an ignorant clod named Tom, denizen of a footloose underworld, happy-go-lucky but doomed. He steps into the jaws of a trap set by God, the trap of an infinitely material universe: here envisaged as a swarm of flies which invade him, breaking down any distinction between self and other, outside or inside. He emerges whole and insane, convinced that the corporeal is the only universe, and that man breathes and lives only as the corporeal universe breathes and lives: that he has no separable existence and partakes of no larger plan: 'filthy blind bastards call Angels men / seeing no further than the forms of men. From which, Tom/Fly begins to gather up the delineaments of a mission: 'confounding all plaguey holiness and righteousness' with 'base things', and thereby 'into majesty'.

Looking for love to make her whole, Maudline, a previously spurned and destitute being, becomes his willing vassal, unaware that her sexuality is a second trap laid by God which will again lure Tom into a descent into blackness. However, this time the blackness will nullify him, strangulating and exterminating the cock-crow of his newly discovered pride. The Lord giveth and the Lord taketh away, and between the giving and the taking lies no difference, only the pure, white malice of unutterable power. *That Slidey Dark* presents its blasphemy straight; even Shift, the supposedly knowing ringside barker, turning the grotesque couplings into gleeful fodder, fails to escape. He ends the play like a rabbit mesmerised by the gleam of God's headlights, his jokes dissolving into an animalesque gurgling as he becomes transfixed by the truth of the void.

After such knowledge, there's clearly no forgiveness, yet there is a kind of hapless residue, born out of the pity we feel for Tom and Maudline: a pity we have to negotiate inside ourselves. We are drawn towards the worldly cynicism of Shift even as that pity sets itself up in our hearts, but we witness his fate and shrink from it. A naked cry is all we have left, something distinctly our own, but also only our own: bereft, and finally useless.

On the surface, *Skin Shanty* seems more diagnostic, in so far as Whitey, the god of *That Slidey Dark*, has shrunk to the proportions of an average white male, deluded and lost but still crazy enough to seek out his victims: all of whom here are female. Perhaps that is what the serial revelations of the pieces are heading towards - an examination of patriarchal power which grows more familiar and yet perhaps more threatening the closer you get to the source. And yet, as we'll see, there is a sting in the tail of this particular devil, a sting that will send the quest off in another, though connected direction. *Skin Shanty* continues to explore mythical dimensions, though one senses here a growing familiarity with his material. Wells is himself a sailor, so there is a platform of reality here, no matter how deep the plunge the play will take. While this again underlines his growing familiarity with his material it also indicates an enhanced riskiness - the closer you get to psychic trauma, the harder it becomes to ride it, to bring back from the twisting patterns of malevolence a shape that might hold. Strangely, almost miraculously, he succeeds.

Skin Shanty's three female sea creatures recall the Fates, but also represent the interlinked worlds of innocence, experience and the consequences of experience. However, the plot is set into motion by Crowforth - without his initiating impulse, their story is as boundless and as fluid as the sea, an admixture of light and dark which sees no need for differentiation. Ezra Pound saw the male will as a "narrow sword of reason" which brought its discriminatory light to beat on the unknowing ceaselessness of the unknowing ocean; but Pound looked for a democratic congress between the two spheres, based on love and an interlinked sense of natural order. Crowforth is the etiolated form of this condition; he seeks the immortality of abstract intelligence of the world through in the binary ping pong of the computer. But he also enacts an older story, embarrassingly close to the vacuity of so much phallic power.

His first love is Teresa, someone glimpsed as a masturbatory gleam in the eye of her demented observer, no matter that she is otherwise real and also disarmingly innocent. Mary Kinney is copulation, actual entrance into the mystery, in whom Crowforth loses himself but from whom he tries to construct a world of meaning and use. And Mags is the dark anima who waits in the wings, a figure of denial and castration, appalled at what the male has made of his experience. Locked in phallic solitude, separated from the flow of the body, man makes of his sterile ivory tower a museum of the spirit, and so dries out, becomes old, brittle and solipsistic. No surprise then, that woman here enacts her revenge, no matter the regret which passes through her being. That stark truth haunts our age and there's little we can do about it; the battle of the sexes has become apocalypse.

In this piece, the women win, their superiority tricked out in a lost language of love. Crowforth becomes a dolly cradled in the murmuring breaths of the deep; he sings an infant song, helpless and dependent, a seed locked in the womb-tomb of the greatest and earliest mystery. And so the play seems to end: but does it? One remembers Teresa's fearful anticipation of Mags and the circular ballad of the play's beginning; one attends to the imagery of the Tomb and womb and one begins to realise that the play forms an enclosed loop, its motions pregnant with the possibility of beginning again, of enacting the same old cycle. This is the sting in the tail to which I referred earlier. The women may win but all they win is the right to fight the same old battle, ad nauseam, until time gives out and even the sea no longer acts as the profoundest measure of our being.

We encounter in *The Glory Reel* an echoing net of rhyme, the net closing upon sense and yet also opening it up: an activity analogous to the play's teasing approach to time. Rhyme looks simultaneously backwards as well as forwards, the meeting of one word with another, a momentary suspension of time's onward thrust. Here we see in miniature a connection to the before and after status of the play's characters, where distinct categories of temporal location are collapsed. They exist in a kind of shifting limbo, a state evoked by the reel itself, which both advances and repeats, seeming to offer variation yet pulled back into repetition, perhaps endlessly.

It is often said that if you repeat a word over and over it loses its meaning. Consider here the repetition of the queue, a word which might indeed begin to lose its meaning, particularly when the text informs us that a queue only leads to another queue, which turn only leads to another. Or consider what might seem an opposing example, namely the numerous transpositions of flack, flock and so on: clearly an attempt to avoid the numbing repetition of the word 'fuck'. Yet what these transpositions attempt to conceal, they also emphatically reveal: a word's stark primacy, hidden in plain sight.

It is through such particulars that the play reveals its complex wholeness. Although it might be argued that the play conforms to a traditional enough narrative, a closer examination disrupts such a response. Caller is bedecked with feathers, and not the scales of a satanic snake; the off-stage deity is a possibly malevolent female. Again, if, this is Limbo, where is the movement towards judgement? And, if these characters are supposedly dead, why do they seem so present, even as they are starting to lose contact with their corporality? And what kind of play is this, which yokes together two characters from two widely divergent backgrounds and genres?

Yet this is a play, not a biblical tract or pulsing western drama. It creates its own reality, teasingly reminding us of a whole range of external references, yet staying stubbornly itself. The play is a fitting conclusion to a strange and compelling body of work. The primacy and power of Nigel Wells's sense of poetry is here extended to the collaborative interplay of music and movement. It was a great pleasure to be present at the creation of these productions.

References

Bailey, Brian, *The Resurrection Men: A History of the Trade in Corpses*. London: MacDonald, 1991.

Barba, Eugenio, and Savarese, Nicola, *A Dictionary of Theatre Anthropology: The Secret Art of The Performer*. London and New York: Routledge, 1991.

Barba, Eugenio, *The Paper Canoe*. London: Routledge, 1995.

Haining, Peter, *The Scarecrow: Fact and Fable*. London: Robert Hale Limited, 1988.

Kennelly, Brendan, *Journey into Joy*. Newcastle upon Tyne: Bloodaxe, 1994.

Kristeva, Julia, *Powers of Horror*. Columbia: New York, 1982.

McCracken-Flesher, Caroline, *The Doctor Dissected: A Cultural Autopsy of the Burke and Hare Murders*. Oxford: Oxford UP, 2011.

Pine, Richard (ed.), *Dark Fathers into Light*. Newcastle upon Tyne: Bloodaxe, 1994.

Wells, Nigel, *Wilderness b/w Just Bounce*. Newcastle upon Tyne: Bloodaxe, 1988.

Wells, Nigel, and Lewis, Caryl, *Walesland/Gwaliadir*. Llandysul: Gomer, 2006.

www.ingramcontent.com/pod-product-compliance
Lightning Source LLC
Chambersburg PA
CBHW080515090426
42734CB00015B/3058